THE CLOSED SHOP
IN
BRITISH INDUSTRY

Stephen Dunn

Senior Lecturer in Industrial Relations
Kingston Polytechnic

and

John Gennard

Professor of Industrial Relations
University of Strathclyde

M
MACMILLAN

First published 1984 by
THE MACMILLAN PRESS LTD
London and Basingstoke
Companies and representatives
throughout the world

Printed in Hong Kong

British Library Cataloguing in Publication Data
Dunn, Stephen
The closed shop in British industry.
1. Open and closed shop—Great
Britain
I. Title   II. Gennard, John
331.88'92'0941   HD6488
ISBN 0–333–26202–6
ISBN 0–333–26203–4   Pbk

To our parents
Alex and Peggy Dunn
The late Arthur and the late Vera Gennard

Contents

List of Tables

Abbreviations

ABS	Association of Broadcasting Staffs
ACAS	Advisory, Conciliation and Arbitration Service
ACTSS	Administrative, Clerical, Technical and Supervisory Staffs of the Transport and General Workers' Union
ACTT	Association of Cinematograph, Television and Allied Technicians
APEX	Association of Professional, Executive, Clerical and Computer Staffs
ASLEF	Associated Society of Locomotive Engineers and Firemen
ASTMS	Association of Scientific, Technical and Managerial Staffs
AUEW(E)	Amalgamated Union of Engineering Workers (Engineering Section)
BOAC	British Overseas Airways Corporation
BRB	British Railways Board
BTC	British Transport Commission
CBI	Confederation of British Industry
CEGB	Central Electricity Generating Board
CPSA	Civil and Public Services Association
DWES	Dockworker Employment Scheme
EEF	Engineering Employers' Federation
ETU	Electrical Trades Union
FBU	Fire Brigades Union
GCBS	General Council of British Shipping
GLC	Greater London Council
GLCSA	Greater London Council Staff Association
GMWU	General and Municipal Workers' Union
IPM	Institute of Personnel Management
IRC	Industrial Relations Commission
IRRU	Industrial Relations Research Unit
ITF	International Transport Workers' Federation
MNAOA	Merchant Navy and Airline and Officers' Association

MNESS	Merchant Navy Establishment Service Scheme
NALGO	National and Local Government Officers' Association
NAS/UWT	National Association of Schoolmasters/Union of Women Teachers
NATFHE	National Association of Teachers in Further and Higher Education
NATSOPA	National Society of Operative Printers and Assistants
NGA	National Graphical Association
NUFLAT	National Union of Footwear, Leather and Allied Trades
NUPE	National Union of Public Employees
NUR	National Union of Railwaymen
NUS	National Union of Seamen
NUTGW	National Union of Tailors and Garment Workers
NUWDAT	National Union of Wallcoverings, Decorative and Allied Trades
POEU	Post Office Engineers' Union
SLADE	Society of Lithographic Artists, Designers, Engravers and Process Workers
SOGAT	Society of Graphical and Allied Trades
SSRC	Social Science Research Council
T&GWU	Transport and General Workers' Union
TUC	Trades Union Congress
TULR(A)A	Trade Union and Labour Relations (Amendment) Act
TSSA	Transport Salaried Staffs' Association
UCW	Union of Communications Workers
UMA	Union Membership Agreement
UPW	Union of Post Office Workers

Acknowledgements

The work on which this book is based began in April 1978, when the authors were members of the Industrial Relations Department of the London School of Economics and Political Science, where the research was carried out. It was completed over four years later, by which time the authors had moved to their present employers. The research was motivated by the fact that while the closed shop had become a subject of fierce public policy debate by the late 1970s it had not been comprehensively studied since the early 1960s. The debate was taking place in a near factual void which we were keen to help fill by investigating the extent, operation and effects of closed-shop arrangements in Britain.

We are grateful to the Department of Employment, Economic and Social Science Branch, which between April 1978 and January 1981 provided the financial support to enable us to undertake this task and which met all our requests for information. During this period our fieldwork was a team effort. Our deep thanks are therefore due to Michael Wright, who as a research officer devoted a great deal of energy to the project and contributed his remarkable diplomatic skills to the problem of securing access to sources of information. When he left in the summer of 1979, he was replaced by a research assistant, Mark Gregory, who fitted admirably into the team and helped in the project's completion. We thank him, Evelyn Cantor, the project secretary, for her part in organizing our programme of interviews, and typing innumerable reports and letters as well as a number of articles, and Philip Dunn, who undertook much of our data processing.

We are extremely fortunate in the co-operation we received from industry. We owe a great debt to the many trade unions, employers' organizations, private companies, local authorities, nationalized industries and other public bodies which spared us their time to answer our inquiries and supply us with information. In particular we are indebted to the Engineering Employers' Federation which undertook on our behalf a survey of one in five of its affiliated establishments. In addition the TUC and the CBI were extremely co-operative in assisting us to gain access to their affiliated members.

For their extensive comments on our work we are grateful to Dr Ray

Richardson of the LSE, Roy Lewis of the SSRC Industrial Relations Research Unit at the University of Warwick, Bill Hawes of the Economic and Social Science Division of the Department of Employment and members of its Policy Division. Nevertheless the views expressed in this book are those of the authors. They do not necessarily reflect those of the organizations and individuals cited above. Any errors remain our responsibility.

A debt of gratitude is owed to Mrs Jean Monaghan, who diligently and cheerfully typed numerous drafts both of our earlier and longer report to the Department of Employment and of this book.

Lastly research work inevitably impinges upon family life and thanks for understanding in this matter are due to Anne, John and Julie Gennard.

STEPHEN DUNN
JOHN GENNARD

1 The Closed Shop: Debate, Policy and the Purpose of this Book

PUBLIC DEBATE

We wrote this book because the one comprehensive study of the closed shop in Britain is now twenty years old. The study is McCarthy's.[1] It has endured well into an era in which, according to piecemeal evidence, the pattern and nature of the practice has changed significantly. A replacement seems long overdue. In attempting to provide it we were inclined to adopt an approach broadly similar to McCarthy's. Like him, we were primarily interested in the perennial industrial-relations themes of job control and job regulation. Consequently our main focus is on the purpose and influence of the closed shop in the relationship between trade unions and management.

Some may argue that this perspective sidesteps the main issue raised by the closed shop. They would contend that the right to dissociate, which the closed shop contravenes, is absolute. It is not contingent upon the needs of trade unions or employers. It is a matter of abstract principles to which industrial-relations activities are irrelevant, even if they can be shown to benefit the individual materially. We could not placate such critics by suggesting that our Chapter 7, in exploring the effect of the closed shop on individuals, may well provide evidence useful to their case. To them numbers are not important. Whether it be a thousand people deprived of their jobs through compulsory unionism or only one, the violation of the basic human right to dissociate is equally unacceptable.

Instead we would defend our approach by pointing to the way in which the contemporary closed-shop debate has been conducted. As Hanson and his colleagues, whose underlying stance appears to be critical of the closed shop, have observed:

Some will perhaps see the problem of the closed shop largely in terms

1

of philosophical arguments about the positive and negative right to associate. Others may be concerned with the custom and practice of labour relations . . . and the balance of economic and political power. But there is no need to be tied to one or other of these different approaches to the problem. They are not mutually exclusive.[2]

Certainly, those who have been drawn to the political battle that has ebbed and flowed around the closed shop during the past twenty years have not allowed themselves to be so tied. Entrenched behind the barbed wire of individualist and collectivist values they may be, but they have not ceased to try to dislodge each other with a bombardment of pragmatic arguments relating to the closed shop's impact on industrial relations.

Let us take examples from each camp. First, the Conservative Party has long couched its opposition to the closed shop in philosophic terms most recently in a 1981 Green Paper which stated 'That people should be required to join a union as a condition of getting or holding a job is contrary to the general traditions of personal liberty in this country . . . Individual employees should have the right to decide for themselves whether or not to join a trade union.'[3] But Conservative politicians have been equally eager to drive home the anti-closed shop message by stressing its detrimental effect on industry, the economy and on workers themselves. As Norman Tebbit, the Secretary of State for Employment, said in October 1982: 'The most privileged trade union movement in the world, commanding a huge conscript army in the closed shop, has failed its members. It has left them near the bottom of the productivity league, condemned them to see their big pay rises wiped out by inflation. It has led them into unemployment . . .'[4] This statement echoes the arguments of those free-market economists who, along with their general reservations about trade unions' power to distort the labour market, have pinpointed the closed shop as a particularly dangerous phenomenon. Its coercive effect is identified in restriction of output, resistance to technological change, retention of outdated skill differentials, shortage of skilled labour, embargoes on the goods and services of non-union firms and damaging use of the strike weapon. The result is escalating production costs, uncompetitive pricing, depressed profit margins and closures. In the long run this means higher inflation and unemployment than would prevail in the practice's absence. Indeed Burton has regarded the problem as sufficiently catastrophic to warrant the state buying out the practice once and for all by means of a lump sum furnished by the issue of a long-term debt before the economy is strangled by a series of union cartels and monopolies.[5]

Second, from the pro-closed shop camp, the moral justification for compulsory union membership is based on the 'common obligation' principle. Admittedly it does not have the philosophical purity of the individual liberty argument, but nor is it merely pragmatic because it does not necessarily imply that the union is any weaker because of the presence of the non-member. Sidney Greene, then General Secretary of the National Union of Railwaymen, described this principle to the Donovan Commission in 1966:

> When I worked on the railway, I was not very pleased when I had paid my contributions and I had done something to improve my conditions on the railway and I might be working next to a chap who was getting the same benefit and was not paying anything at all . . . The real reason for the closed shop is to see that everybody on the basis of equity should make a contribution to collective bargaining.[6]

Traditionally trade unionists have referred to those who shirk this common obligation as 'free riders', carried on the backs of their unionized workmates. But once the pragmatic industrial-relations arguments are added, the name changes to 'blacklegs', with far more bitter connotations. The non-member is seen not merely as selfish or feckless, but as an employers' collaborator who undermines union solidarity, breaks the strike, crosses the picket line, undercuts the union rate and dilutes the craft. The closed shop has been the means by which this threat to union organization and bargaining power was eliminated. The turbulent history of many of our traditional industries provides the evidence, none more graphically than coal-mining. McFarlane quotes the old Durham ballad 'The Blackleg Miner':

> O don't go near the Sedgehill mine
> Far across the mainway they hang a line
> To catch the throat and break the spine
> Of the dirty blackleg miners.
>
> So join the union while you may
> Don't you wait till your dying day
> For that may not be too far away
> You dirty blackleg miners.[7]

McCarthy's own justification of the closed shop twenty years ago was based on trade unions' experience in such industries. He saw the practice as a significant means by which unions sought to match employers' bargaining power and thus protect and improve the conditions of workers whose individual power relative to the employer was negligible. He identified three specific problems that trade unions might have found difficult or impossible to tackle without the imposition of compulsory membership and that stimulated its members to coerce fellow workers into the union or to exclude non-unionists from the job. These were:

(a) the problem of organizing the workforce, where the closed shop could help overcome obstacles presented by high turnover, geographical dispersal, fear of employer retribution and competition from other unions, and in so doing performed a membership function
(b) the problem of controlling the workforce, where the closed shop could help reinforce union discipline, especially when employer hostility created the need for strike solidarity and the unilateral imposition of working rules; here the practice performed a discipline function
(c) the problem of organizing and controlling the alternative workforce, where the substitution of union members by other workers, whether elsewhere in the company or on other occupations or from the ranks of the unemployed was the threat and where the closed shop performed an entry control function.

While accepting this analysis as an historical defence of the practice, contemporary apologists of the closed shop have doubted its efficacy today. They see it as too vulnerable to accusations that the closed shop is an anachronism and that in a period when unions are far more tolerated by employers the three functions have now become methods of union oppression in industry and society. Instead they have sought to sway the debate by tackling boldly in the opposite direction. The closed shop, they suggest, has metamorphosed into an aid to achieving orderly well-regulated industrial relations to the benefit of industry and workers. Moreover, they have found evidence from management to support them. For example, Cliff Rose, Personnel Director of British Rail, wrote in 1980 that:

in my view and experience, there is also a major positive motivation factor present in some [closed shop] cases. Responsible collective bargaining is about reaching agreement on pay, conditions, working practices and so on and about delivering those agreements on both sides. Some trade union leaders believe they are better able to deliver their side of the agreement in an environment of compulsory union membership by being able to discipline members who act unconstitutionally.[8]

This statement almost exactly mirrors the academic reappraisal of the closed shop during the 1970s which culminated in Hart's article entitled 'Why Bosses Love the Closed Shop'.[9] In it she identified the practice as a useful component in the reform of workplace bargaining, the success of which depended upon the shop-floor conforming with formalized agreements and procedures and union officials and shop stewards being sufficiently insulated from shop-floor pressures to be able to take unpopular negotiating decisions relating to, say, productivity and rationalization. By making union membership compulsory, the closed shop locked the rank and file into the union disciplinary machinery, strengthened it by linking withdrawal of union card with loss of job, prevented protest resignations and defections to more populist unions, and thus increased the authority and confidence of union representatives.

These illustrations are sufficient to indicate how philosophical and pragmatic arguments have been employed by both sides in the closed-shop debate. But we suggest that, because of this, a problem has arisen that makes the need for a detailed study of the industrial relations of the closed shop especially important. The problem is one of polarization. As the philosophical arguments represent opposite poles, industrial-relations evidence has been attracted to one or the other like iron filings scattered between two magnets. The result has been a tendency to present the closed shop's role in industry as decisive; to convey it as a monolithic institution working for good or ill depending on point of view: 'A closed shop is a closed shop is a closed shop.' Even before we began our research, our instincts and experience as industrial-relations academics told us that this was unlikely to reflect industrial reality. One of the dilemmas we faced in designing our project was that merely by isolating the closed shop as our field of study we would inevitably be prone to magnify its significance. After all, we were not studying the difference between strong unions and weak unions. We were engaged in the far more intricate task of distinguishing between the industrial behaviour of those for whom union membership was a condition of employment and those for whom membership was voluntary. Admittedly this would involve encounters with strong unions with closed shops and weak unions without them. But it would also bring us across weak unions with closed shops and strong ones without them. For instance, both coal-miners and shop assistants are covered by closed shops. Is that an important similarity in understanding their industrial behaviour? And in comparing the Union of Communications Workers (UCW) (formerly the Union of Post Office Workers), which operates a closed shop, with the Post Office Engineering Union, which does not, although it has achieved nearly 100 per cent voluntary membership, how is it possible to disengage the closed shop from a host of other variables that determine the similarities and differences in the way they operate? It would be folly to maintain that the UCW must be more militant merely because it has a 'conscripted' membership, or indeed that it co-operates more fully with management for the same reason. Yet the closed-shop debate has often been conducted in these terms, ignoring considerations as union strategic position, membership homo-geneity and union consciousness, the traditions of industrial relations in the industry or firm, and the frequency and type of issues that generate conflict with management during the work process and in job regulation.

We cannot claim to have completely overcome the problem of magnifying the closed shop in relation to the complex processes that surround it. Even if we had, it is doubtful whether it would have prevented the two camps from selectively plundering our work for ammunition. Already the Report to the Department of Employment – the so-called Gennard Report[10] – upon which this book is based, as well as previously published elements of our research,[11] have been used by both sides of both Houses of Parliament in debate. This we accept is the public purpose of our research. It was publicly funded and becomes public property, especially when conducted against a background of legislative change. However, before we outline these public policy developments – an essential precursor to the main body of the book – it is important to emphasize that our aim here has been to indicate the elusiveness, intricacy and ambiguity of the closed shop's industrial role which has tended to be lost when the moral blackening or whitening of compulsory unionism spills over into pragmatic judgements.

PUBLIC POLICY

Before the 1971 Industrial Relations Act there were no statutory provisions regulating the closed shop although there had been some important judicial decisions concerning the practice. In 1924 in *Reynolds* v. *The Shipping Federation* the Court of Appeal held that the closed-shop agreement between the seamen's union and the employers' federation was legitimate as showing 'a desire to advance the business interests of employer and employed alike by securing or maintaining those advantages of collective bargaining and control'. Eighteen years later the House of Lords adopted a similar line in *Crofter Hand Woven Harris Tweed* v. *Veitch* when it held that 'all parties were pursuing their legitimate interests, the mill owners to increase their control of the market and their profit, the union to improve wages and extend membership – all to create a better basis for collective bargaining'. In 1966 the House of Lords in the case of *Faramus* v. *Film Artistes Association* acknowledged the need for the regulation of employment in the film industry provided by the union's rule book and the closed-shop arrangement.

However, the judgement in *Rookes* v. *Bernard* (1964)[12] called into question the immunity of trade unions from legal action when threatening to call strikes in support of the closed shop. To deal with this uncertainty the government passed the Trades Disputes Act 1965 which sought to plug this loophole and appointed a Royal Commission under the chairmanship of Lord Donovan to examine the whole industrial-relations system and to recommend changes in the law, including that concerning the closed shop, if felt necessary.

The Donovan Commission reported that 'in our view the closed shop as it operates at present is not always in the best interests either of workers or of the community as a whole. It is liable from time to time to cause substantial injustice to individuals from which they have no effective means of redress. It also contributes to the maintenance of a system of training that is out of date or inadequate to the country's needs'.[13] However, it concluded that the closed shop should not be prohibited since prohibition could not be made effective, and that it was better to recognize that with proper safeguards a closed shop could serve a useful purpose and that alternative means of overcoming the disadvantages that accompanied it should be devised. To this end it recommended that there should be a right to complain to an in-dependent review body if a trade-union member felt he had been unjustifiably expelled, had suffered damage in consequence, or had any penalty inflicted upon him by the union which amounted to a substantial injustice. The Commission, however, was unenthusiastic about the closed shop on economic grounds and accepted it could result in adverse economic effects.[14] Government intentions to give effect to these recommendations fell with the defeat of the Labour administration at the 1970 general election.

Although the promotion of collective bargaining was one of its stated aims, the incoming Conservative government's Industrial Relations Act 1971 was nevertheless concerned to protect individual rights. Where these conflicted with collective interests, it was the intention that favour should be given to those of the individual. The Act declared the pre-entry closed shop void and gave workers a statutory right to join or not to join a trade union. It made provision for the continuation of closed shops only in very special circumstances. Such arrangements were permissible where they were necessary to maintain organization, reasonable terms and conditions of employment and reasonable prospects of continued employment; to promote or maintain stable collective bargaining arrangements and to prevent collective agreements from being frustrated; where an agency shop could not reasonably be expected to fulfil the same purposes and only if the workers affected by the proposed agreement did not apply for and hold a secret ballot which failed to approve the agreement by the required majority. The provision was intended to enable the British Actors' Equity Association and the National Union of Seamen to continue their pre-entry closed shops as long as they allowed conscientious objectors to pay contributions to charity instead of union dues. More generally the Act introduced the concept of the agency shop whereby a registered trade union could secure the financial support of all employees within a defined area, even though individuals were given the right, while paying for the services provided by the union, to choose not to be a member.

When a Labour government was returned in 1974, its own philosophy that public policy should be designed to promote collective bargaining did not exclude the closed shop from that task. Its Trade Union and Labour Relations Act 1974, which repealed the Industrial Relations Act 1971, nevertheless developed the unfair dismissal legislation introduced in 1971 and sought to accommodate the closed shop within it. It made the dismissal of an employee for non-membership of a trade union in a closed shop fair except in the case of a worker who genuinely objected to any trade-union membership whatsoever on religious grounds, or who objected on any reasonable grounds to membership of a particular trade union. The Trade Union and Labour Relations (Amendment) Act 1976, however, narrowed the grounds of automatic unfair dismissal for non-union membership in a closed shop to genuine objections to being a member of any trade union because of religious belief. The passage of this Act was a matter of political controversy, which almost ended in a constitutional crisis between the Lords and the Commons. Most of the safeguards in the 1974 Act were introduced by the Liberal and Conservative Opposition against the minority government's wishes. Achieving a majority in October 1974, Labour pushed through the removal of the 'reasonable grounds' safeguard only to meet opposition from the House of Lords so stubborn that the government was almost forced to invoke the 1911 Parliament Act.

By the end of the 1970s the closed shop was causing increasing controversy among politicians, press, the public, employers and the trade-union movement over the issue of individual rights, and trade-union power. The change in government in 1979 brought legislative reform intended to satisfy the practice's critics, although the Conservative administration did not resurrect the 1971 right not to belong to a union. Instead its main legal thrust tightened the unfair dismissal restrictions. The 1980 Employment Act sought to ensure that closed shops were established only with the wholehearted support of the workers concerned and that there was a remedy for abuses of individual rights in their operation. The Act extended the protection against dismissal for non-membership of a union in a closed shop: (i) to those who object on grounds of conscience or other deeply held personal conviction to being a member of any trade union whatsoever or a particular trade union, (ii) to existing non-members on the introduction of a closed-shop agreement, and (iii) to all employees if the closed-shop agreement came into operation after 15 August 1980 and it had not been approved by at least 80 per cent of those covered voting in a secret ballot. It also enabled the employer to require the trade unions to 'be joined' as a party to any such unfair dismissal case and be wholly or partly liable for any compensation awarded. Protection for the individual working in or seeking employment in a closed-shop area was further extended through the right not to be arbitrarily or unreasonably excluded or expelled from union membership. Finally, the Act gave the Secretary of State authority to issue a statutory Code of Practice giving advice, based on current best practice, on introducing and applying closed shops.

In November 1981 the government announced further legislative proposals concerning the closed shop. Introducing the proposals the Secretary of State said the government's aim was twofold. First, the proposed measures were designed to safeguard the liberty of the individual from the abuse of industrial power, and second to improve the operation of the labour market by providing a balanced framework of industrial-relations law. Thus the Employment Act 1982 widened the reasons for which dismissal for non-union membership in a closed shop was automatically unfair. From 1 November 1984, unless support for a closed-shop agreement or arrangement has been reaffirmed in a secret ballot within the previous five years, dismissal for non-union membership in a closed shop is to become automatically unfair. This also became the case, although protection was immediate, where an employee at the time of dismissal either had been found by an industrial tribunal to have been unreasonably excluded or expelled from the trade union to which he was required to belong under the closed-shop agreement or had a complaint of unreasonable exclusion or expulsion by that union pending before a tribunal. The same protection applied to an employee who had qualifications relating to his job that made him subject to a written code of conduct and who either had been expelled from his trade union because he had refused to strike or to take other industrial action on the grounds that this would have breached his code of conduct, or had refused to belong to the union concerned on the grounds that membership would have required him to take industrial action in breach of the code.

In addition to increasing the number of circumstances in which dismissal for non-union membership became automatically unfair, the 1982 Act attempted to influence the operation of the closed shop through the level of and liability for financial compensation in the case of proven unfair dismissals. The Act enabled a complainant to require there to be joined as a party to the unfair dismissal proceedings any person (including a trade union) who allegedly exerted pressure on the employer to dismiss him by calling or threatening industrial action because he was not a union member. Furthermore, the Act aimed to provide a powerful disincentive to an employer who was tempted to dismiss an employee unfairly in order to enforce a closed-shop agreement. This took the form of a substantial increase in the level of compensation available in such circumstances. Under the Act, if an individual did not seek reinstatement then the basic compensation award was, unless subject to reduction on account of the individual's behaviour, subject to a minimum of £2000, plus a compensatory award based on loss of earnings in the past and the future and loss of pension rights, subject to a maximum of £7000. However, if an individual sought reinstatement, the Act made provision for additional components of compensation, called Special Awards. If the tribunal did not make a reinstatement or re-engagement order then

the special award was to be two years' pay subject to a minimum of
£10 000 and a maximum of £20 000. If a reinstatement or re-engagement
order was made but the employer failed to comply with it the amount of
the special award was to be three years' pay subject to a minimum of
£15 000.

The two Employment Acts further attempted to deal with practices
related to the closed shop but that fell outside the unfair dismissal
framework. Blacking of non-union produced goods and services with the
explicit purpose of recruiting workers into a certain union or unions was
made unlawful under the 1980 Act unless the action was aimed at other
workers employed by the same employer or workers who worked at the
same place. The 1982 Act contained measures designed both to counter
the use of clauses inserted into commercial contracts requiring that work
should be carried out only by union members, and the refusal of
employees to handle goods produced by non-union labour.
Furthermore, it removed trade-union immunity from legal action in
cases where a person took industrial action against an employer on the
grounds that work was or was likely to be done by workers employed by
another employer who were, or were not, members of a trade union.

The legal developments relating to the closed shop are further
discussed throughout the book, especially in Chapters 3, 4, 7 and 8.
However, the above summary provides sufficient background to enable
us to begin our analysis of the growth, operation and impact of the closed
shop in Britain during the past twenty years.

2 The Closed-shop pattern: Mid-1978

INTRODUCTION

In Britain the definition and identification of the closed shop is not a simple matter. Definition may depend on the purpose for which it is needed. For example, some employers and trade unionists prefer to regard a closed shop as 100 per cent compulsory union membership in order that an arrangement with which they are associated might avoid the stigma of being classified as a closed shop. This may be true where certain employees – existing non-members or those with a conscientious or religious objection to union membership – are allowed to remain outside the union. Our own definition is wider and generally accepted since it follows McCarthy's view that a closed shop is 'a situation in which employees come to realise that a particular job is only to be obtained or retained if they become and remain members of one of a specified number of trade unions'.[1] This, we feel, allows us to include arrangements in which not every employee comes to such a realization. In short, 100 per cent membership is not a prerequisite for a practice to be included under the closed-shop label.

Identification problems are not so easily resolved. Few difficulties exist where union membership as a condition of employment is specified in a formal collective agreement between union(s) and management. But often the practice exists in custom and practice only and is regulated with varying degrees of informality and management involvement. Under such circumstances it is sometimes difficult to ascertain whether areas of long-established 100 per cent union membership are *de facto* closed shops. Where a union attempts to enforce a closed shop unilaterally on an unwilling management there may be disagreement between the two sides over the degree of compulsion involved in ensuring workers belong to the union. Even where management participates in the administration of monitoring 100 per cent union density, for example by operating the check-off system, the situation may not be recognized as a closed shop because of the absence of a test case to decide whether non-union membership will result in dismissal from employment. If job applicants do not refuse to join the union, if employees do not lapse, tear up their union cards, or are not expelled from the union, and if trade-union membership has become a deeply ingrained habit, then the issue of whether a closed shop exists in a workplace may lie dormant for years. Whether a closed shop can be said to operate in this instance depends on the extent to which employees realize, when union, and perhaps management, pressure is exerted upon them, that failure to take up or maintain union membership would in the end result in a loss of job.

In conducting our research some reliance was placed on an acknowledgement by interviewees that an informal closed shop operated in a certain area. In general, managerial acceptance of a *de facto* closed shop was taken as evidence of its existence. Nevertheless a managerial denial was not necessarily regarded as sufficient to classify a grade or establishment as an 'open' shop. Where possible verification was sought from trade-union sources and when the two sides disagreed, we were left to weigh up the evidence and make a judgement. Difficulties in identifying informal closed shops means that our estimate of the extent of the practice must be considered a minimum figure.

DATA COLLECTION

The information upon which this book is based was collected over a period of three years beginning in April 1978. To calculate the number of workers affected and to assess the impact of the closed shop two methods were used. First, for some industries information was based on 250 interviews conducted with representatives of both sides of industry. Contact was made with senior industrial-relations managers in central government, local authorities, the nationalized industries, the water authorities, the health service and over one hundred private companies. In addition, interviews were conducted with senior officials of twenty-six employers' associations, and ninety individual trade unions.[2] Second, for some industries data were derived from postal surveys to a representative cross-section of firms, supplemented by interviews conducted on both sides of industry. Postal surveys were undertaken of 1200 establishments affiliated to the Engineering Employers' Federation,[3] of 120 local authorities in Great Britain, of the six Passenger Transport Executives in England and a number of holding companies whose industrial relations were decentralized. In addition, the research team also had access to data collected by other academics working either directly or indirectly on the closed shop.[4] From these sources reliable information was obtained about the extent of the practice among 19 million of the estimated 22 million employees in employment in mid-June 1978.[5]

THE CLOSED-SHOP PATTERN: MID-1978[6]

Types of Arrangements

In Britain the closed shop is usually divided into two types. The first is the *pre-entry* closed shop under which an individual has to be accepted as a union member before being considered for employment. The essential feature of pre-entry closed shops is control over the supply of labour to the firm at the point of hiring. The method by which this is done varies. First there is the labour supply shop in which the union office is recognized as the sole or main supplier of labour and operates as a labour exchange. Second, there is the labour pool shop under which employers recruit from a recognized pool of labour confined to workers accepted into membership by the unions. Once an individual has secured entry to the pool he has freedom to move from one job to another without reference to the union. Third, there is the promotion veto shop in which seniority of union membership determines the ordering of promotion to higher-status jobs. Finally, there is the craft qualification shop by which craft unions or sections of unions restrict membership to those who have completed an apprenticeship or similar training and limit the number trained in this way through, for example, an apprenticeship ratio.

The pre-entry shop is much rarer than the *post-entry* which does not attempt to control the supply of labour to the firm at the recruitment stage. Under such arrangements, the employer is free to take on a non-unionist, so long as he joins the union shortly after taking up the offered employment unless he has an acceptable objection. The vast majority of the closed-shop population is covered by this type.

The Number of Workers in Closed Shops

Table 2.1 shows that closed-shop arrangements affected at least 5.2 million employees in Great Britain in mid-1978, or 23 per cent of workers. This compared with McCarthy's figure of $3\frac{3}{4}$ million workers

TABLE 2.1 *The extent of the closed shop: coverage at mid-1978*

Industrial order	No. of employees June 1978 (000s)	No. of workers covered (000s)	% covered by survey	No. known to be in closed shop (000s)	% of workers covered by survey in closed shops	Minimum % of total workforce in closed shop
I Agriculture, forestry and fishing	377	360	96	3	1	1
II Mining and quarrying	341	296	87	296	87	87
III Food, drink and tobacco	696	500	72	266	53	38
IV Coal and petroleum products	36	30	83	20	67	55
V Chemical and allied	429	325	76	137	42	32
VI Metal manufacture	459	370	81	228	62	50
VII Mechanical engineering	925	786	85	412	52	45
VIII Instrument engineering	147	118	80	16	13	10
IX Electrical engineering	740	629	85	220	35	30
X Shipbuilding and marine engineering	175	145	83	99	68	57
XI Vehicles	764	650	85	369	57	48
XII Metal goods (not elsewhere specified)	537	460	86	178	39	33
XIII Textiles	464	330	71	100	30	21
XIV Leather, leather goods and fur	40	36	90	6	15	14
XV Clothing and footwear	365	300	82	83	28	23
XVI Bricks, pottery, glass, cement	263	190	72	88	46	33
XVII Timber and furniture	259	195	75	76	39	29
XVIII Paper, printing and publishing	537	445	83	354	79	66
XIX Other manufacturing	328	270	82	137	50	41
XX Construction	1 219	1 086	89	89	8	7
XXI Gas, water, electricity	340	335	99	273	81	80
XXII Transport and communications	1 426	1 150	81	798	69	56
XXIII Distributive trades	2 683	2 200	82	397	18	15
XXIV Insurance, banking and business finance	1 134	920	81	52	6	5
XXV Professional and scientific services	3 575	3 200	90	126	4	3
XXVI Miscellaneous services	2 364	2 140	87	132	6	6
XXVII Public administration and defence	1 586	1 300	82	226	17	14
Total	22 209	18 766	84	5 181	27.6	23.3

or 16 per cent of the workforce for the early 1960s. Our figure must be regarded as a minimum, not only because of the identification problems outlined above but because in certain industries, notably construction, it proved difficult to obtain firm data. The figure given for construction in Table 2.1 is based solely on reliable information and in practice is likely to be an underestimate.[7]

McCarthy revealed that five industries – coal-mining, iron and steel, engineering, shipbuilding, and printing–accounted for almost two-thirds of his closed-shop population. Between 1962 and 1978 the total workforce in these industries declined by 20 per cent compared to an average across all sectors of 2 per cent. Had there been no spread in the industrial distribution of the closed shop since the early 1960s, in 1978 the closed-shop population would have been 2.9 million. Thus there was a net growth in the closed-shop population over this period of at least 2.3 million. The spread into 'new' industries in the manufacturing sector accounted for 30 per cent (or 700 000) of the net growth. The biggest contributions were made by food, drink and tobacco, clothing and footwear, chemical and allied industries and coal and petroleum products.[8] More significant, however, was the increased penetration of the closed shop into the nationalized industries. A quarter of the total closed-shop population was found to be in these industries and three-quarters of employees in them were covered by some type of closed-shop arrangement or agreement. The spread of the closed shop here accounts for about 40 per cent of the net closed-shop growth over the last two decades.

Since the early 1960s the closed shop has also become more familiar in white-collar employment. In 1978 there were at least 1.1 million non-manuals in closed shops compared to 300 000 in the early 1960s.[9] The practice, however, remained predominantly a feature of manual employment where at least 30 per cent (4.1 million) of the total workforce were covered by some kind of closed-shop arrangement.[10]

A minority of the closed-shop population (837 000 or 16 per cent) was in pre-entry shops. By 1978 the numbers in labour supply shops had dropped from 141 000 to 74 000 since 1962, in labour pool shops from 145 000 to 72 000 and in promotion veto shops from 193 000 to 127 000. In each case the explanation lay in declining employment in the industries involved. The craft qualification shop was, however, more problematical. Whereas McCarthy placed 167 000 workers in craft qualification shops and another 104 000 in uncategorized pre-entry arrangements, our residual population, once the first three types had been excluded, was 569 000. This raised our total pre-entry population from McCarthy's 750 000 to 837 000, which was surprising since we discovered no large groups of workers who had succeeded in establishing new pre-entry shops since 1964. The discrepancy is explained by differences in identification of the extent of diluted forms of the craft qualification shop.[11]The dominant single pre-entry closed-shop industry was paper, printing and publishing, Only 5 per cent of the pre-entry closed-shop population were non-manuals of whom 80 per cent were in entertainment and related industries.

Almost all the spread in the practice over the past two decades was accounted for by new post-entry arrangements. Although the majority of workers that came to be so covered were manuals there was a significant proportion of white-collar workers affected. They accounted for 25 per cent of the total post-entry closed-shop population. In the early 1960s the post-entry closed shop was highly concentrated in two industries – coal-mining and engineering – but by mid-1978 the practice had become more widespread. This trend was more evident for manual workers than for non-manual.

The Form of Closed-shop Arrangements

The tendency is to use the term 'formal closed shop' to describe a written collective agreement covering compulsory union membership and to use the term 'informal' for any other kind of closed-shop arrangement. However, matters can be complicated since the title 'union membership agreement' (UMA) is commonly used in reference to formal/written closed-shop arrangements, although the legal definition of a UMA under the Trade Union and Labour Relations Act (TULRA) 1974 and Trade Union and Labour Relations (Amendment) Act (TULR(A)A) 1976 covers both formal (written) and informal (unwritten) agreements. To avoid any confusion, in this chapter the term formal closed-shop agreement refers to arrangements that are subject to a written collective agreement between unions and management. Any other type of closed-shop arrangement is classified as informal, including where pre-entry shops operate, as in printing, through formal union rules which tend not to be ratified on the employers' side by a joint agreement.[12]

Table 2.2 shows that 54 per cent of the closed-shop population were covered by written agreements. The trend towards greater formality in the practice began in the late 1960s. The move was temporarily slowed by the Industrial Relations Act 1971 which drove existing formal arrangements underground[13] and ensured that new closed shops were not committed to paper. Its repeal was accompanied by a spurt of formal

TABLE 2.2   *The extent of the closed shop: formal v. informal arrangements at mid-1978 (figures to nearest 000)*

Industrial order	Formal shops Pre-	Formal shops Post-	Informal shops Pre-	Informal shops Post-	Total Pre-	Total Post-
Agriculture, forestry and fishing	—	2	1	—	1	2
Mining and quarrying	—	96	—	200	—	296
Food, drink and tobacco	—	195	11	59	11	254
Coal and petroleum products	—	15	1	4	1	19
Chemical and allied	—	55	62	20	62	75
Metal manufacture	—	47	33	148	33	195
Mechanical engineering	9	126	70	208	79	334
Instrument engineering	—	11	2	3	2	14
Electrical engineering	1	16	52	107	53	123
Shipbuilding and marine engineering	—	30	64	6	64	36
Vehicles	16	131	49	173	65	304
Metal goods n.e.s.	—	96	11	71	11	167
Textiles	—	49	33	17	33	66
Leather, leather goods and fur	—	4	2	—	2	4
Clothing and footwear	—	77	6	1	6	78
Bricks, pottery, glass, cement	—	29	5	55	5	84
Timber and furniture	—	14	21	41	21	55
Paper, printing and publishing	—	42	176	136	176	178
Other manufacturing	20	86	8	22	28	108
Construction	—	10	5	74	5	84
Gas, electricity and water	—	273	—	—	—	273
Transport and communications	59	521	22	186	91	707
Distributive trades	—	374	20	3	20	377
Insurance, banking, finance and business services	—	52	—	—	—	2
Professional and scientific services	—	115	3	8	3	123
Miscellaneous services	—	73	44	15	44	88
Public administration and defence	—	127	20	79	20	206
Total	1 15	2 666	721	1 636	836	4 302

closed-shop agreements that only began to slacken in 1978. *De facto* arrangements were formalized and pre-1971 agreements were re-activated, while almost all new agreements took written form. The industries where informality still predominated were those where traditional practices had not been converted.

Some have attributed the movement towards formal closed-shop agreements to changes in the legal status of the practice under the Trade Union and Labour Relations Act 1974, its 1976 Amendment, and the Employment Protection Act 1975.[14] However, our research showed that this movement began to gather momentum before these legal changes and before the passage of the 1971 Industrial Relations Act. Of those companies contacted that had formal closed-shop arrangements, nearly 60 per cent had concluded at least one of them prior to 1971. Over 70 per cent of these had negotiated their first agreement between 1965 and 1971, the concentration being towards the end of the 1960s when formal arrangements began to supplant informal ones as the preferred form of closed shop.

Initially formalization was stimulated by a more general movement towards comprehensive procedural and substantive agreements, especially at plant level as advocated by the Donovan Commission. The pattern was, however distorted by the 1971 Industrial Relations Act. Evidence suggests that companies began widely adopting the Donovan proposals in the early 1970s.[15] Yet between 1971 and 1974 the law prevented closed-shop arrangements keeping in step with the developing formality in other aspects of plant industrial relations. By the time TULRA made the practice a legal possibility, the degree of formality in closed shops was lagging behind that of other practices[16] and there was a flurry of activity to bring their status into line or to revive previous agreements which, in theory, if not in practice, had lapsed, during the period of the Act.[17]

The Trade Union and Labour Relations Acts themselves have had some impact on the trend towards formal closed-shop agreements. The changes in unfair dismissal legislation with repsect to union membership brought about by these Acts meant management began to examine their closed-shop arrangements to avoid legal pitfalls. A number decided that this could be best done by tightening up and formalizing existing arrangements.

The Level at which Closed Shops Operate

Closed-shop arrangements in the private sector are most frequently based on the workplace within which there may be separate agreements/arrangements for different occupational groups, for example, skilled, unskilled, clerical and administrative. However, within the private sector there exist highly complex bargaining structures and if a general rule can be established it is that closed-shop arrangements and agreements tend to operate at the most local level possible which usually means plant or sub-plant level. A formal agreement might cover all the manual workers on a site except skilled workers who may be covered by an informal pre-entry arrangement. A second might cover all the supervisors and a third all the clericals. There are of course numerous deviations from this general pattern. In multi-plant companies it tends to be more common for white-collar unions to negotiate on a multi-site basis, concluding either company- or division-wide agreements. A further group of employees often covered by formal agreements that extend across plant boundaries are lorry drivers, but unlike white-collar workers their arrangements frequently developed out of informal practices that drivers had developed on a multi-location basis by virtue of their mobility.

Apart from decentralized bargaining units an important factor in the local nature of closed-shop arrangements is a consideration on the part of management and unions that the practice is a matter best handled at local level where particular obstacles can be adequately dealt with, whether they relate to individuals or inter-union relationships. Where corporate industrial-relations departments have sought to impose consistency across their organization they have generally confined themselves to establishing broad policy guidelines to be followed by local management, that is, the provision of a model agreement. In an attempt to compromise between centrally imposed uniformity and local diversity a small number of companies, particularly in the textile and clothing industries, have concluded enabling closed-shop agreements with their unions. These are in effect model agreements that are jointly agreed outside the plant. They lay down what criteria must be fulfilled before a formal post-entry closed shop can be 'triggered' at a location. Once these are satisfied the closed shop is implemented automatically upon a request by the local unions without further negotiation. Our research found that few multi-plant private-sector firms had attempted to negotiate formal closed-shop agreements at the company level. The exceptions tended to be companies such as Ford and ICI with determined policies to establish and/or maintain centralized industrial relations.

The problems encountered in negotiating a formal closed shop on an industry-wide basis are many. Not only do the negotiators have to consider uneven patterns of union growth and variations in industrial-relations practices at the level of plant and company but the ideological and practical objections of individual employers. Union demands for the closed shop to be concluded at this level have been common[18] but discussion has been more contentious than within companies or plants. Few industry-wide formal closed-shop agreements have resulted.[19] These occurred in relatively small isolated industries with distinctive characteristics including a strong employers' association whose collective agreements are adhered to by member firms and a single industry-based union whose commitment to the national bargaining machinery is similar to that of the employers. By virtue of this commitment employers and union officials have been able to sustain and consolidate their influence over local industrial relations and have both restrained the development of company or plant autonomy and facilitated a uniform growth in union membership.

With a few exceptions, by far the biggest bargaining units are in the public sector. As a result, in the nationalized industries, for example, a handful of closed-shop agreements negotiated at corporate level covered well over 1 million workers. However, some of the more recently created public corporations, for example, British Steel, British Aerospace and British Shipbuilders, have retained elements of their pre-nationalization diversity in industrial-relations practices and have not attempted to impose a uniform closed shop across the corporation. British Steel, for example, has negotiated an enabling agreeement similar to those found in textiles.

The Content of Closed-shop Arrangements[20]

The contents of 136 formal closed-shop agreements were analysed. They were drawn from eighty separate employers and included thirty-three agreements, covering 1.2 million workers from the public sector and 103 agreements covering 0.5 million from the private. As managements supplied one or two union membership agreements typical of company practice, the sample reflected closed-shop arrangements involving a far greater number of employees than the 1.7 million directly affected.[21] We are confident that they are representative of formal closed-shop agreements in British industry.

Although the agreements varied considerably in detail and working there was standardization in broad subject matter covered. Formal closed shops tended to divide those within their jurisdiction into three broad categories, namely: (i) new entrants to the group covered by the agreement, (ii) existing union members at the time of the introduction of the agreement, and (iii) existing non-union members at the time of the agreement's introduction. In addition, such agreements contained procedures to deal with problems that may have arisen from their operation. Frequently, the procedures distinguished between those cases in which the individual acted in contravention of the agreement by, say, resigning from the union and those cases in which the union acted against individuals by withholding membership or expelling them. The precise outlining of the three broad categories, their rights, and obligations and the procedures by which such rights were safeguarded and obligations enforced, meant that the typical formal closed-shop agreement was three or four pages in length, often with attached schedules, notes for guidance, and recorded minutes of the negotiations clarifying the 'spirit' in which the agreement was to operate. This was in contrast to the one-clause statements typical of those formal agreements existing in the early 1960s.[22]

Ninety-six per cent of the sample agreements required that new employees entering their jurisdiction join an appropriate union. The commonest period within which membership was to be taken up was four weeks. While an obligation on new entrants to join the appropriate union was common to all but six of the agreements, the majority (82 per cent) allowed at least one ground upon which new employees might avoid union membership. A high proportion of agreements excluded existing employees from union memberships if they objected to it on religious grounds. Non-manual agreements placed greater emphasis on exempting new entrants from union membership on grounds of the post they were to occupy. Such exemptions occurred in a third of white-collar agreements as opposed to 8 per cent of blue-collar. These jobs included secretaries to certain directors and managers, various specialists including employees in the personnel department and those concerned with safety where potentially dangerous processes were involved. In most cases those holding such posts were free to join and remain in the union but were not compelled to do so.

The vast majority of agreements examined stipulated that employees already in membership at the time of the agreement's implementation should generally continue in membership as a condition of employment. Nevertheless, all except seven agreements contained provision for non-continuity of union membership on at least one ground. The most common was religious belief but others included part-time or temporary employment, existing membership of a non-signatory union to the agreement, conscience, training, and employment in a key or senior post. The commonest type of agreement in the sample was that which, with certain exceptions, made union membership a condition of

employment solely for new entrants and existing members, placing no
obligation on existing non-members to join the union. Two-thirds of the
agreements reviewed excluded existing non-members from their provisions, leaving one-third that stated that union membership was
obligatory for all employees, but again with exceptions, for example,
religious belief and part-time work. Over half of these tight agreements
were formalizations of closed-shop practices stretching back at least to
the 1960s, and the lack of protection for existing non-members was
because there were none.

Of the 136 agreements, 77 laid down special procedures over and
above the normal dispute procedures solely to handle problems arising
from their implementation and operation. Forty-nine of these made
provision for an independent arbitrator as the final stage, binding in
honour on the parties involved. In addition, thirty-five of the seventy-
seven agreements contains a clause prohibiting any form of industrial
action against an individual under appeal or against the company
during the operation of such procedures. Apart from these seventy-
seven, a further forty-one referred closed-shop issues to the ordinary
disputes procedures. A substantial proportion of the sample included an
even more specialized procedure to deal with cases of exclusion and/or
expulsion from the union. In 29 per cent of agreements examined the
TUC Independent Review Committee was mentioned as the appropriate arbitration body for exclusion/expulsion cases. If the number of
agreements mentioning the Committee was taken as a proportion of all
the agreements signed since 1976, when the Committee was established,
then the percentage figure increases to 33.3. All these elaborate
procedures appeared to have been seldom, if ever, used. Out of the
eighty companies covered by the agreements, only thirteen claimed to
have used their special procedure on one or more occasions.

To sum up, during the late 1960s and the mid-1970s agreements
appeared that defined precisely the obligations and rights of workers
where union membership existed as a condition of employment. For
example, it was the norm on the introduction of a new closed shop to
exclude existing non-unionists from compulsion to join the union, and
for agreements to contain procedures specifically designed to handle
difficulties arising from its operation.

3 The Pre-entry Closed Shop

Because the pre-entry closed shop has long existed in such industries as printing, dockworking, merchant shipping and in a host of skilled trades, it is often assumed that it represents an unassailable bastion of trade-union power. Certainly, the pre-entry shop offers unions much greater job control than the post-entry variety. Yet this hides its essential fragility. It develops out of the vulnerability of workers to a substitute labour force. Once established, it provides the union concerned with control over entry into jobs that are often of strategic importance in the production process and in so doing increases its potential to enforce working rules unilaterally and drive up wages. Yet the successful imposition of a pre-entry shop on a trade or industry, although it may gain employer toleration, will usually provoke a challenge in the longer term. The employers eventually tend to react to the loss of prerogative and the higher wage costs by seeking a new alternative workforce over which the existing pre-entry shop exerts no control. Such alternative workforces can be created or tapped by the introduction of new production techniques that undermine existing skills and jobs, and by 'runaway' to a location outside the jurisdiction of the pre-entry shop.

If successfully adopted, this strategy represents a critical threat to the union's organization and industrial influence. Indeed its continuance as an effective protector of its member's interests may be in jeopardy. Its response has to be immediate if it is to re-establish itself as a viable force within the new production environment. Radical changes in methods of operation, recruitment and industrial regulation may be necessary, including in some circumstances the abandonment of an exclusive membership base delimited by pre-entry restrictions in favour of a comprehensive post-entry strategy involving the incorporation of as many of the alternative workforce as possible into the union. Success is not guaranteed.

In this chapter our main emphasis is on this dynamic. As illustrations we use the merchant shipping, dockworking and printing industries where traditional labour pool, labour supply and craft qualification shops have come under increasing threat in recent years.

THE LABOUR POOL SHOP

Merchant Seamen

In merchant shipping the closed-shop arrangements for manual grades take the form of joint union–management control over the size and distribution of the labour force.[1] The details of this joint control have been adequately described elsewhere and need not be repeated here except to note that the Merchant Navy Establishments Service Scheme (MNESS) is financed by a levy on firms in membership of the employers association for merchant shipping (The General Council of British Shipping). Those seeking employment at sea approach the Local Administration Office and register with the MNESS. The prospective rating must join the NUS before gaining admission to the register. The size of the pool of manual labour is determined by the demand for labour and the adjustment of the register in the appropriate direction is jointly agreed by the employers and the union. To match the needs of shipowners a rating may be transferred from one office to another for allocation to a particular ship. However, in recent years there has been a growing trend towards seamen being continuously employed by one company rather than returning to the pool between voyages. Before sailing, seafarers sign the ship's article of agreement which sets out the terms and conditions of employment aboard the ship. To do so they must show good standing with the NUS.

During the 1960s Britain ceased to be the world's major maritime nation. By the end of the 1970s it was in fourth place and the number of ships sailing under the UK flag had dropped from 2319 in 1966 to 919 in 1982. This had been caused by a number of factors, notably technological developments and the growth of 'flag of convenience' vessels.

Over the past two decades technological developments have resulted in the rise of the supertanker, and traditional cargo vessels facing increased competition from bulk carriers and containers vessels. There was a marked decline in the number of passenger vessels owing particularly to the rise of relatively cheaper air transport. These developments brought about a change in the employment structure of the industry. By the late 1970s the majority of the workforce in merchant shipping was non-manual. Ships were increasingly run by technicians and officers without the need for large numbers of ratings. Other developments affecting the employment of ratings were the growth of flag of convenience ships, the use of Asian crews on ships flying the UK flag, and the withdrawal of companies from the General Council of British Shipping.

The trend of shipping companies to transfer the registration of their vessels to other countries, particularly developing nations, began soon after the end of the Second World War. However, in the 1970s this trend gathered pace,[2] and by 1980 ships carrying a flag of convenience accounted for 25 per cent of the world's total merchant fleet and were expected to rise to 35 per cent by the mid-1980s. The advantages of the system include attractive fiscal arrangements, low registration fees, and lower manning costs made possible by the absence of trade unions and closed-shop arrangements. The main countries to which shipping companies have transferred ownership are Liberia, Panama, Cyprus, the Bahamas and Bermuda. Liberia now has the largest merchant fleet in the world. Parallel to the growth in flags of convenience fleets has been the growing practice of employing on them seamen from developing countries at lower rates of pay than prevail in Europe and North America. For example, vessels registered in Hong Kong are able to recruit local seafarers who command wages at only a quarter of the UK average rate for seamen. The late 1970s and early 1980s saw an increasing number of ships flying the UK flag being transferred to a flag of convenience and thus out of the NUS–GCBS closed-shop arrangements. On page 29 we discuss a recent case involving Cunard's passenger liners. The flag of convenience issue compounded a long-term problem encountered by the NUS relating to the comparatively low wages paid to 'non-domiciled' crews. Traditionally, British flag vessels have employed Asian crews at Asian rates on Far Eastern trade routes. Foreign crewing goes back to the British Raj when cheap Indian labour was employed because British ratings could not be found to man the ships. The NUS was prepared to accept this while the UK merchant fleet was expanding. However, in the depressed state of the industry in the late 1970s and early 1980s the union came to see the use of Asians as a threat to the future employment prospects of its members. For the shipowner Asian crews meant a considerable reduction in crew costs. In 1982 a British seaman earned around £147 per week while an Asian was paid only £78 per month.[3] Nevertheless in 1975 the NUS and GCBS made an agreement governing the employment of Asian crews on ships flying the UK flag whereby the employers paid a per capita levy to the union for each Asian crew member employed.

The early 1980s saw 25 of the then 185 member companies withdrawing from the General Council of British Shipping and hence from the closed-shop arrangements. The companies concerned were small coastal-shipping lines and an important reason behind the defederation was to avoid the levy the GCBS charged to administer the Merchant Navy Establishments Service Scheme. The withdrawal of companies from the scheme meant that the financial cost of the closed-shop arrangements increased for those who remained in membership. The NUS feared that the competitive advantage to be gained from not having to pay the levy and to abide by terms and conditions of employment agreed between the NUS and GCBS would be an incentive to other firms to leave the system. It was also feared that defederated firms might operate as non-union concerns.

The effect of the developments described above has been a steady fall in the NUS membership from 62 500 in 1965 to 45 000 in 1970 and to 35 000 in 1982. In an attempt to try and control these alternative workforces the NUS has adopted collective bargaining and political lobbying policies which, if successful, would bring into its jurisdiction work that has been able to bypass its control in recent years.

The NUS has sought to control the growth of flag of convenience vessels through participation in the International Transport Workers' Federation (ITF) campaign to enforce acceptable union standards in ocean transport throughout the world.[4] The objective of the campaign has been to ensure that wages and conditions of seafarers on flag of convenience ships are adequate and to force all ships back to the flags of those countries in which genuine control of the vessels lies, and thus employment back to the members of the maritime unions of those countries. The ITF has pressurized the International Labour Organization and national governments to introduce appropriate legislation, and has sought to negotiate agreements (called blue certificates) with shipowners covering acceptable ITF wage and safety standards for crews of flag of convenience ships. These agreements are made, in many instances, under an actual or threatened boycott of a vessel. By the early 1980s the ITF claimed to have concluded over 1000 blue certificate agreements but the extent to which these have eliminated the comparative labour cost advantage of a flag of convenience and brought work back to NUS members and employees back into the closed shop net is difficult to assess. The effectiveness of the ITF's campaign, based on boycott activity, depends on supportive national legislation with respect to secondary action and the willingness of affiliated and allied unions to take such action.

The 1982 Employment Act, by redefining a trade dispute to cover only disputes between employers and their own workers, seemed likely to make the ITF policy against flags of convenience more difficult to pursue. The effect of the changed definition of a trade dispute in section 18 of the 1982 Act was that a union could not lawfully take action against an employer unless some of that employer's own employees were in dispute with him. Thus, so long as some seamen on a flag of convenience ship were in dispute with their employer then the ITF could call on them to take industrial action. It was possible that secondary action by the ITF could meet the provisions of section 17 of the 1980 Employment Act although it would depend on the details of the case. The first test in examining the legality of industrial action was whether there was a trade dispute. If there was no trade dispute, there was no immunity. From this point of view, section 18 of the 1982 Act was fundamental. If any ITF action fell at the first 'trade dispute' hurdle, section 17 of the 1980 Act was irrelevant. Section 17 only became relevant if it had been first established that a lawful trade dispute exists.

The NUS has been involved in industrial action to prevent UK shipowners transferring their vessels to a flag of convenience. In September 1981 Cunard announced the transfer of two of its three passenger liners, the *Cunard Countess* and the *Cunard Princess*, to the Bahamian flag. Over 200 British seamen were to be replaced by cheaper foreign ratings. In October the crew of the *Cunard Princess* began a sit-in that prevented the ship leaving Barbados while the NUS ceased supplying new crew members to Cunard ships and asked members already employed by the company not to report for duty. After failure to reach agreement, the NUS called a national one-day stoppage for 3 November and an indefinite strike in all Cunard vessels as and when they entered port. The company threatened to sell all three ships if the union continued to oppose its plans to transfer them to a flag of convenience. On 6 November a settlement was reached under which the *Princess* was transferred to the Bahamian flag but the *Countess* remained UK-registered and retained its existing crews.

The NUS has not seen industrial action and participation in the ITF boycott campaign as sufficient to arrest the decline of its members' employment. Political lobbying activities have also been undertaken. The union hoped the European Economic Community would ban flag of convenience ships from its ports. It has urged, without success, UK governments to ban all but British flagged ships from operating around its coasts and in the North Sea oilfields. In the UK oilfields more than 50 per cent of such vessels are foreign ships with foreign crews. The NUS has estimated that a ban on foreign ships and crews in the North Sea would create an extra 2000 jobs.

Despite the 1975 manning levy agreement, the NUS has attempted to control Asian crews on UK-flag ships by pressing for such crews to be paid at the same rate as British crews when they were employed on UK owned ships. The policy has been unsuccessful not least because Asian trade unions and the Indian government feared that the payment of UK wage rates threatened their own members' employment opportunities. Under the 1975 Agreement the GCBS paid the NUS £15 per head a year for every Asian seaman employed on a ship flying the UK flag. At that time they were estimated to be 22 000 Asians employed on British ships and although by 1983 the number had fallen to 5500, of which 3200 were Indians, the levy at £30 per head was generating £175 000 per annum for the union's fund, that is, some 10 per cent of its income. In March 1983 the NUS gave notice to the GCBS that from 30 September 1983 it was terminating this Asian manning levy agreement. It was unlikely that this NUS decision would create any additional jobs for their members since owners were likely to get round the ending of the agreement by changing to a flag of convenience or simply by selling their ships. The employers claimed that paying British wage rates in the future would make their freight rates uncompetitive.

The union reacted to the growth of firms withdrawing from the employers' associaton by negotiating individual company agreements coverning pay and union membership. A non-federated sector of larger firms had always operated in the industry and here the NUS secured closed-shop agreements and negotiating rights. It hoped to make similar deals with firms that withdrew from the GCBS in the early 1980s. It has had success with the larger firms, for example, North British Shipping, but experienced difficulty with the smaller ones. The union remained fearful that a significant non-union sector paying wages below those agreed for the industry might develop in the 1980s.

Dockworkers

The Dock Labour Scheme was introduced in 1947 under the Dock Workers (Regulation of Employment) Act 1946. The management of the labour force is vested in the National Dock Labour Board and local dock labour boards on which both sides of the industry are equally represented. Establishment on a register entitles the docker to a basic minimum wage and to perform dockwork as defined by the port. A docker established on a register is in continuous employment even though he may not work all the time. The 1946 Act was designed to reduce the casual nature of employment but complete decasualization did not come until 1967, when under the Dock Workers Employment Scheme (DWES) registered dockworkers were permanently allocated to employment with individual registered port employers.

Before a worker can obtain employment in a DWES dock he must be accepted for registration by a local board which in practice means applicants must secure membership of the appropriate local union branch. The register divides dockworkers into a number of different categories.[5] Each has a 'sanctioned strength' which is adjusted periodically according to the labour requirements of the industry. If demand increases a number of unregistered workers may be allowed to enter the docks on temporary engagements. Natural wastage is expected to take care of a permanent fall in labour demand since registered dockworkers cannot be made redundant. This protection springs from an undertaking given by the employers at the time of decasualization rather than from any statutory provisions. Temporary release schemes allow dockers released to find work elsewhere to be placed on a 'dormant register', but voluntary severance schemes provide an incentive for dockers to leave the register permanently. In 1969 a national voluntary redundancy scheme resulted in 12 000 men leaving the industry over a two-year period while in 1972 a special voluntary severance scheme, run for six months, resulted in more than 8000 leaving the industry. However, over-manning still exists in the registered ports which over the past fifteen years have accounted for a decreasing proportion of total trade passing through all UK ports.

In 1967, 57 000 workers were covered by closed-shop arrangements for registered dockworkers. By 1982 the number had fallen to just over 15 000 and the National Association of Port Employers forecast a fall to 14 000 by the end of 1984. This erosion was largely the result of port and related employers introducing more capital-intensive production methods such as containerization, roll-on roll-off and mechanized cargo handling, and the growth of trade through ports outside the jurisdiction of the Dock Workers Employment Scheme. The unions in the registered ports have attempted to retrieve this loss of work and regain control over the supply of labour to the port transport industry.

The Dock Labour Scheme defined dockwork and its boundary was drawn around the ports. Within it only a registered docker could handle cargo. Outside this boundary the docker had no such rights. This legal definition of dockworkers ran into difficulties when technological developments resulted in cargo handling no longer being confined to the waterfront. The docker's work could now be performed in an area where he had no monopoly job rights. In the early 1960s technological developments centred on increasing the flow of work through the port and did not take it out of the hands of registered dockers. Packaged timber, bulk sugar and forklift trucks reduced the employer's demand for labour but did not remove handling from the boundaries of the registered ports. On the other hand, the development of roll-on/roll-off services and the introduction of containerization were dramatic for the registered dockworker. With roll-on/roll-off services, a 'truck from Wolverhampton could drive to Hull, board a ferry and unload in Denmark, or could detach its trailer which could be collected by a lorry at its destination. The impact of the container was more dramatic. It required only a handful of men to move it on and off ships while the most labour-intensive of dockwork – namely, packing and unpacking – could be done outside the area of the port. The container was designed to pass through the docks without being opened. Traditional dock facilities were inappropriate for containers and new productive capacity had to be established such that much dockwork moved inland from traditional docking areas.

When the registered scheme was introduced in 1947 many ports were excluded because they were considered too small to support a regular labour force. However, the statistics of port growth in the last twenty years show that conventional ports like London and Liverpool declined sharply, that in medium-sized ports trade growth varied but that explosive growth rates were found in the small ports, most of which were outside the registered scheme.[6] There was a steady growth in the number of dockers employed outside the DWES. Indeed by 1982 there were 6000 dockers working in over eighty unregistered ports, which handled 20 per cent of seaborne trade. The growth of trade outside the registered ports reflected a shift in UK trade patterns which resulted in a decline in the west coasts ports – predominantly registered – to the benefit of those ports on the south and east coasts which were mainly outside the DWES. However, factors other than geography were at work and the non-registered dock employers have cost advantages in that they do not have to contribute a fixed proportion of their wage bill to fund the administration of DWES. When a registered firm closes, moves premises or leaves the scheme, its former employees are reallocated among those employers that remain. This adds to their costs, generates pressure for increases in charges and puts future trade and jobs at risk. The unregistered port employer does not face these pressures.

To regain dockwork lost through technological change and the movement of trade to unregistered ports, dockworkers have sought to obtain from Parliament a redefining of dockwork, to black containers and to persuade unregistered employers to join the DWES. A key issue concerned the legal definition of 'dockwork'. Dockers' demands centred on extending the boundaries within which they would have the right to perform dock- and related work. Although a legal definition of dockwork was contained in the 1946 Act, the Docks and Harbours Act 1966 changed the method of determining dockwork. Under this Act disputes were referred to an Industrial Tribunal but between June 1968 and January 1970 only one out of nineteen such disputes was defined as work to be performed by registered dockworkers. Although the number of job losses from these decisions was small, the implication of the judgements was that any new port investment entailing charged forms of work could be removed automatically from the DWES. The fear of the dockers was summarized by Wilson.

> With industrial sense running a poor second to strict legality, dockers soon gave up hope of extending their working rights through the law. They saw shipowners and port employers building container groupage depots first outside the vicinity of the ports and employing non recognised labour; their predictable reaction was to forsake the Industrial Tribunal and turn to industrial sanctions.[7]

The change of tactics was first witnessed in 1969 when Liverpool shop stewards called a strike to have work in the Aintree container base, less than 2 miles from the port, reserved for registered dock labour. In November 1969 a similar dispute at Hay's Wharf threatened to close the whole London docks. The dispute led to the establishment of the Bristow Committee, consisting equally of employer and union representatives, to re-examine the definition of dockwork in London. It proposed a new definition of dockwork to include any number of handlings by dockworkers within the port and to extend the boundaries of the London docks to a proposed corridor 5 miles wide on each side of the Thames. Although the recommendation was never implemented the issue of the definition of dockwork came to the fore in 1972 when dockers in Liverpool laid claim to all stuffing and stripping of port-load containers no matter how far inland the work had been done. They insisted that all consignments be brought inside the dock-gate and registered dockers then stuff them. In the case of import containers dockers demanded that they be stripped on dockland premises. The Liverpool 'blacking' led to a national strike in the summer of 1972.[8] As part of the settlement of the dispute the Aldrington-Jones Committee was established to inquire into the industry's problems and recommended that container work should as far as possible be carried out by registered dockworkers but, if by other workers, then only under conditions of work prevailing in registered docks. Such agreements were sought with establishments that previously employed dockworkers but since 1967 had moved outside a registered port. London port authorities responded to the recommendation and a few extra jobs were obtained for registered dockworkers.[9]

As regards non-registered ports and wharves the Aldrington-Jones Committee recommended the government to take action if by September 1974 a significant problem of sub-standard working conditions remained in these areas. They argued that the registered ports should not be exposed to unfair competition on terms and conditions of employment from ports and wharves outside the DWES. In July 1974 the government announced its intention to extend the DWES to commercial ports not already covered; to apply the scheme not only to dockwork but to all port transport work; to enable the scheme to be expanded, on the advice of the Dock Labour Board, to cover new areas or other groups; to make arrangements that the ACAS Central Arbitration Committee ensure the employment conditions of no one within the new 'portwork' definition were less favourable than those of comparable workers in the district; and to transfer jurisdiction over disputes about the boundaries of dockwork/portwork to the Central Arbitration Committee. To this effect the Dock Work Regulation Bill was presented to Parliament in 1975. By the time it emerged as an Act in 1976, its original proposals had been a considerably watered down. An envisaged concept of a cargo handling zone had been replaced by a 'definable dock area' the coverage of which was reduced to half a mile around the port areas alone. Although the Secretary of State was given powers to extend the area by order it was to be only after a long consultation procedure the final stage of which was approval by a House of Commons resolution. In 1978 a new Dockwork Regulation Scheme to replace the 1967 one failed to receive parliamentary approval. Since this date there have been no new attempts by Parliament to introduce a new dockwork employment scheme.

In 1982, however, the registered dockers changed tactics to gain control of alternative workforces by demanding that the DWES be extended to all ports and wharves. Previous demands centred on extending the boundaries of registered ports within which dockers had the exclusive right to perform portwork. The dockers in registered ports called for a national dock strike from 10 May 1982 unless the government agreed to talk over the extension of the DWES to all non-scheme ports and wharves. The government rejected a blanket extension of the DWES but agreed to consider 'specific and detailed proposals' for particular ports and wharves. By October 1982 the union had approached eight of the eighty plus non-registered ports seeking their agreement to a joint approach to the government for their inclusion in the 1967 scheme. All rejected the request on the grounds they would import the alleged labour inefficiency encouraged by the scheme and they did not wish to pay the levy to the National Dock Labour Board for the administration of the scheme.

THE LABOUR SUPPLY AND CRAFT QUALIFICATION SHOPS

The recognition of the union as an employment agency is the distinguishing feature of the labour supply shop. It is found in parts of the textile industry, in the London wholesale markets and a variety of small trades.[10] But it is seen in its most developed form in the recruitment of craft, semi-skilled and certain white-collar workers in the national newspaper industry. Since earnings in this sector are much higher than elsewhere in the industry there is usually a queue for vacancies and a waiting list is administered by the unions concerned. The procedure is well documented and need not be repeated here.[11]

Craft qualification shops exist among apprentice-trained skilled workers in many industries. Indeed it is common to find such pre-entry arrangements wherever small pockets of skilled maintenance personnel are employed to service semi-skilled production processes because management finds it convenient to accept a craft union card as evidence of experience and competence. Such informal practices are too scattered and widespread to enable the unions concerned to retain any strict control over the craft. Even in engineering, where there is a long tradition of craft control, the sheer size of the skilled workforce and the fragmented structure of the industry has precluded the operation of an apprenticeship ratio and has allowed a leakage of dilutees into skilled grades. Hence some of the pre-entry arrangements that exist are vulgarized versions of the pure craft qualification shops and are best described as 'union qualification' shops. Their essential feature is that the job applicant, by either apprenticeship or some dilutionary means, has managed at some point to obtain the appropriate union card.

Again it is in printing and provincial newspapers that the craft qualification shop operates in its tightest form. The National Graphical Association (NGA) has been able to insist upon apprenticeship ratios through a system jointly regulated with the British Printing Industries Federation and the Newspaper Society. This has been an integral part of the NGA's control over the printing process by the following classic methods. First, the union restricted the number of apprenticeships available. Second, it confined membership to those who had served an apprenticeship. Third, it defined and protected jobs exclusive to the NGA members – commonly referred to as 'traditional areas'. Fourth, it monitored movement within the traditional areas by means of the credential and clearance card system.[12] Fifth, it regulated the hiring of casual labour in Fleet Street, especially to prevent oversupply and hence the undermining of wage rates. And sixth, it obliged its members to refuse to handle work originating from and going to non-union printing offices outside the NGA's jurisdiction.[13] A similar system was used by the former SLADE, in the area of design and illustration, except that through its 'white-card' procedure, the union maintained a tighter control over the filling of vacancies, giving priority to unemployed members.[14]

The 'traditional areas' that the NGA protected by the above methods were the composing and reading rooms, the foundry and the machine room. On either side of these areas other unions and/or unorganized workers were to be found. Feeding 'origination work' to composing rooms involved members of NATSOPA (clerical), the National Union of Journalists (NUJ) and the Institute of Journalists, or more often non-unionists. At the 'back end', completed NGA work was distributed mainly by SOGAT[15] members (see Figure 3.1).

Although this traditional method of printing remains in many firms, new technology, in which provincial newspapers have set the pace,

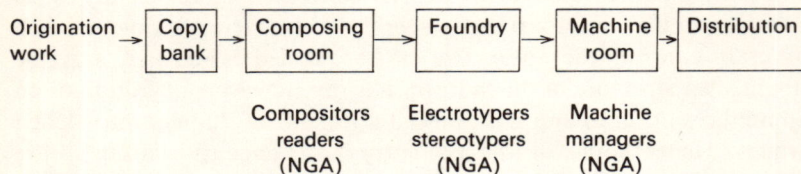

Origination work	→	Copy bank	→	Composing room	→	Foundry	→	Machine room	→	Distribution
				Compositors readers (NGA)		Electrotypers stereotypers (NGA)		Machine managers (NGA)		

FIGURE 3.1

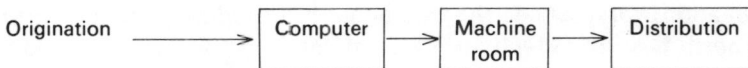

FIGURE 3.2

profoundly affects the NGA and the former SLADE by threatening to eliminate traditional jobs performed by their members. For example, in newspapers employers have introduced direct entry systems under which it is possible for journalists and sales staff to keystroke into computers that automatically prepare materials for printing and thereby usurp the functions of the composing room (see Figure 3.2).

The new printing techniques require only a short period of training, as evidenced by the growth of an 'alternative' printing industry that consists of in-plant printing, instant print shops, in-plant origination by publishers, art studios and advertising agencies. Work can now be done by less skilled people and may be performed on premises where terms and conditions of employment are inferior to those prevailing in many traditional printing firms.

Even more profound is the decline of the 'old world' of communications based on paper and ink, which the NGA dominated, and the rapid rise of a 'new world' based on information technology, for example, local radio, Ceefax, Oracle, Prestel, video, cable and satellites. In this 'new world' the NGA has only a precarious foothold. The input of information is in the hands of either non-unionized workers and such diverse unions as the NUJ, the ABS, ACTT, POEU, and the Banking, Finance and Insurance Union. If the NGA were to fail to colonize this 'new world', its viability would be in doubt.

Painful though it has been, the NGA had been increasingly forced to relinquish its craft exclusiveness and traditions in order to maintain control in the shrinking 'old world' and to gain access to and influence over the 'new world'. Its strategies have included:[15]

1. *New technology agreements* in the 'old world' designed to ensure that origination input remains within the NGA job territory regardless of the skill involved in the job. Often this has involved management agreeing to double key stroking which for the NGA offers a temporary means of defending existing craftsmen's livelihoods.

2. *Attempts to return work to traditional printing firms* by a rigorous enforcement of Rule 43 which forbids members to handle work from unrecognized sources. This 'blacking' strategy again encounters the obstacle of the 1982 Employment Act, and also has brought the Association into conflict with unions whose members are performing

origination work outside the traditional print industry. NALGO, for example, has over 1400 members doing such work in the local authorities.

3. *Attempts to organize new groups of workers.* The NGA has tried to recruit unorganized workers in art studios and advertising agencies, where the more robust activities of SLADE attracted public attention and a government-sponsored inquiry.[17] The NGA was more selective, not seeking to impose post-entry closed shops in any company where employees were opposed to it. Within the traditional printing industry, the Association decided in 1980 to attempt to extend its membership base into the relatively unorganized non-manual occupations. This initiative stemmed from a small industrial union, NUWDAT transferring its engagements to the NGA and giving the Association the expertise it lacked as a craft union to recruit in white-collar areas. In this expansion it is adopting the classic union progression for recruitment, recognition, negotiating rights and finally a *post-entry* closed shop.

4. *Attempts to amalgamate with unions in both 'worlds'.* Trying to retain its hold on the 'old world', the NGA has sought a merger with the NUJ, 40 per cent of whose membership is in 'the print' where under new technology journalists' key stroking replaces the composing room as the nerve centre of the production process. The fact that organization among journalists is low and employers have strongly resisted their closed-shop demands is an incentive for the journalists to merge with the NGA, their combined strength being seen as the means of eroding non-union key stroking. The NUJ also provides a bridge to the 'new world' for the NGA in so far as it has membership in such areas as broadcasting, press and public relations and common interests with others such as ABS and ACTT and other media unions that the NGA lacks. In June 1981 the NUJ and NGA began formal merger talks that were broken off in the spring of 1983 after reaching an advanced stage. The Association has responded to this breakdown by entering amalgamation discussions with SOGAT 82, following an earlier successful merger with SLADE (March 1982). Were the SOGAT talks to be successful, the NUJ's membership in the 'old world' would be isolated against one big print union. Their pressure in the case of this isolation might force the NUJ to reopen marriage negotiations.

5. *Attempts to maintain control of labour supply in the 'old world'.* While accepting that new technology has dramatically affected the training needs of the industry, the NGA has sought to retain some control over the volume and selection for trainees by means of a revolutionary 'Recruitment Training and Re-training Agreement' with

the BPIF in 1983 which replaced apprenticeships with a modular system of training allowing skilled status to be achieved in no more than two years. Even so, the principle of employer/union regulation of the number of new entrants was retained. From August 1983 all recruitment and training needs were to be based on manpower plans drawn up by individual companies and chapels. Only if these needs could not be agreed at this level was a regressive training ratio to be imposed on the company, depending on its size. In this event trainees would not attain craft status for at least three years.

CONCLUDING REMARKS

This chapter shows that three classic pre-entry closed shops whose impact on the industry concerned was decisive have since McCarthy's study began to be eroded by technological change and managerial evasion strategies. Thus, while these closed shops are often held up as examples of entrenched union restrictive practices, they are in fact in danger of crumbling. Although the unions concerned have adapted to crisis in the past, the challenge today is far more fundamental and requires a profound readjustment in outlook, policy and strategy if they are to retain or re-establish their regulatory grip on the new environment. We have outlined the response of the unions concerned but at this point it would be rash to predict their outcome.

4 The Growth of the Post-entry Closed Shop since the mid-1960s: Theoretical Framework[1]

This chapter and the next attempt to explain the rise of the post-entry closed shop since the early 1960s. We begin by constructing from published material and inductive reasoning two discrete, although not mutually exclusive, theories. These are tested against data derived from our field survey in Chapter 5. The first, which we call the 'hard theory', states that the post-entry closed shop spread because trade unions, employers or both identified it as having a significant impact upon industrial relations from which they were likely to gain substantial advantages. The second, which we call the 'soft theory', states that in contrast the post-entry closed shop spread almost as a side-effect of other industrial-relations developments which reduced its significance and therefore its contentiousness as an issue between unions and employers.

THE HARD THEORY

Any explanation of closed-shop growth involves determining why trade unionists seek such arrangements and why employers allow their establishment. But it is insufficient merely to produce one checklist of union reasons for wanting a closed shop and another of managerial reasons for accepting it. The two must be linked in an explicable way.

McCarthy had made this link. He classified the closed shop primarily as a trade union weapon which, by offering unions significant advantages in organizing and controlling the workforce, was likely to increase their bargaining leverage. Identified as such, the practice was likely to be accepted by the employer only under duress.[2] In other words, the spread of the closed shop was a matter of power. It depended upon union pressure, often in the form of strikes, or similar sanctions or the threat of them, forcing the employer to concede on the issue.[3] Hence, looking at the closed-shop pattern as it existed at the beginning of the 1960s, McCarthy observed that, although most trade unions could appreciate the benefits of the closed shop, not all were in a position to achieve it. Many unions that needed it to overcome problems of membership retention or of recruiting a scattered workforce were precisely those that had never been capable of mustering sufficient collective strength to break down employer resistance. Equally, there were some unions, notably in the public services, whose organization in depth seemed sufficient to sustain a successful closed-shop campaign but whose institutional security was sufficient to render such a campaign superfluous to their needs. They had never bothered to pursue the issue vigorously and operated effectively on a voluntary membership basis. Their members might have resented non-members as 'free riders', but they lacked 'an additional readiness to take positive collective action'[4] to eliminate them. That left the closed shop unions. These possessed both the solidarity and the motivation to persevere against employer opposition until compulsory union membership was agreed. McCarthy found them clustered in a relatively few trades and industries, where craftsmen had striven to impose unilateral working rules and to resist skill dilution, where union organizers had fought running battles with employers to prevent them tapping an abundant supply of casual labour as an alternative to unionized workers, and where strikes and lockouts had become common tactics in collective bargaining.[5] In short, the closed shop had tended to appear in sectors where industrial relations had been hardest. Here, trade unionists had identified non-unionism as a menace and had forged the solidarity necessary to combat it.

How far is McCarthy's analysis relevant to the post-entry closed-shop growth over the period mid-1960s to 1980? The answer depends upon two factors:

(1) the amount of evidence to suggest that industrial relations has generally become harder in Britain over the past twenty years to the extent that more and more trade unionists have appreciated the value of the closed shop as a practical means to achieve the solidarity necessary in such circumstances.

(2) the amount of evidence to suggest that unions have been able to translate this appreciation into collective action sufficiently forceful to push employers into accepting the closed shop.

If sufficient evidence on both counts could be mustered, then McCarthy's analysis would remain valid. The dynamics of closed-shop growth would remain the same: a union perception of the advantages of the practice; an employer perception of its disadvantages; and a trial of strength to determine who prevails.

In support of the first, it might be argued that the relative deterioration of the British economy after the mid-1960s has influenced the industrial-relations system to a critical degree. On the one hand, unions have sought to maintain and enhance their members' living standards in the face of accelerating inflation and unemployment.[6] On the other, employers have attempted to cope with tightening market constraints by control of labour costs and by greater productivity while the state has offered incomes policy and legislation as a means of restraining union activities.[7] One result has been a significant increase in industrial conflict. Working days lost through strikes in the 1970s exceeded those lost in any decade since the 1920s. Such strikes involved more workers and they tended to last longer.[8] In such circumstances it might be surmised that trade unionists would have found the additional security and solidarity offered by the closed shop to be of benefit. Where workers have had little experience of striking, its use as an instrument of discipline to stiffen resolve when disputes drag and enthusiasm wanes would reinforce McCarthy's contention that 'the relationship between the closed shop and strike action is one of the most important factors in explaining the closed shop pattern'.[9]

While a prima facie case along the above lines might be made in support of the first count, the second presents difficulties. Requiring evidence of employer hostility towards the closed shop and resistance to its establishment, we find instead evidence that employers' attitudes towards the practice moderated during the period under consideration. They became more amenable to union requests to introduce the closed shop. Indeed they were increasingly prone to see its advantages to them. Admittedly, McCarthy did not discount the fact that managers might see some benefits once a closed shop had been operating for a while. But he did not think that they were sufficiently persuasive to alter the deep suspicion that employers felt when faced with a closed-shop demand.[10] By the 1970s, however, observers were placing greater emphasis upon the closed shop as a managerial device[11] to the extent that, by the second half of the decade, it became established academic currency that managers approved of the practice and, in firms where trade unionism was accepted and catered for, seldom offered a great deal of resistance when a union presented a closed-shop claim. For example, Hanson *et al.* explain the latter-day growth of the closed shop without reference to trade-union needs, stressing instead management gains.[12]

In part, the shift in managerial attitudes has again been associated with deteriorating economic conditions. For employers the harsher climate has made order in industrial relations a priority. To achieve it, so one argument goes, they abandoned the indulgent strategy adopted towards unionized workers during the boom years of the 1950s and 1960s in favour of a *corporatist* strategy that attempted to use union officials and institutions, including the closed shop, to help in the task of controlling the rank and file and shaping its behaviour to fit prevailing market constrictions.[13] In the private sector, under the influence of the Donovan Report,[14] the dominant tendency was towards formal bargaining relationships with union officials and particularly shop stewards at plant level and the negotiation of comprehensive workplace agreements. The hope was that these agreements would diminish the importance of custom and practice and discourage unconstitutional strikes. By elevating shop stewards to a formal, legitimized position within the plant and by facilitating the development of steward hierarchies, management further hoped that stewards' authority would be strengthened in the interests of such agreements.[15]

Hart identified the closed shop as an important component in this kind of reform. She saw it as underpinning the authority vested in union officials and stewards by creating a settled territory into which rival unions could not penetrate and out of which dissident members could not escape. Enjoying such security, union representatives, she argued, had more confidence to conclude unpopular agreements and to take a harder line with groups who broke procedure than they did in an open shop.[16]

This analysis of post-McCarthy closed-shop developments presents a paradox. One argument suggests that the growth of the closed shop since 1964 was connected with increasing union militancy in an increasingly unfriendly economic environment. The other suggests that it was connected with a managerial search for order and stability in the same environment. It is no longer possible to assume the continued relevance of the McCarthy theory. Indeed a new formula would seem to present itself, that is, union perceptions of the closed shop's advantages plus employer perceptions of its advantages equals agreement. Is such a formula explicable? Could both sides in the same situation have identified substantial gains from the closed shops? If not, we would be forced to say that there may have been two strands of closed-shop growth in latter years. In some contexts, the closed shop has appeared as a trade-union weapon with which to belabour the employer, in others a mangement tool to manipulate the workforce, and never the twain shall meet; while to an extent that may have been so, a theory of closed-shop growth based on two neatly divided and contrasting paths would seem inadequate. However, a more integrated theory based on the second formula can be defended, but it requires an understanding of the collective-bargaining relationship.

Collective bargaining resolves conflict not only by coercion, but also persuasion. At the bargaining table threats may be made, but equally negotiators need to play their cards close to their chests, revealing only information that appeals to the other side and that minimizes the gulf between them. Otherwise the process cannot develop into a search for common ground, nor a system of joint regulation. In the course of closed-shop negotiations, for example, the expectation would be that the union would focus discussion not on facets of the practice that management is likely to find unpalatable but on those that offer mutual benefits: notably the avoidance of inter-union problems and the control of dissidents. It would be naïve to assume that management is incapable of calculating the extent to which the closed shop would contribute to union solidarity in a dispute. But nor could it be assumed that, in making such a calculation, management would find this cost prohibitively high. Given that the everyday problems of industrial relations tend to involve short, unconstitutional sectional disputes and inter-union wrangles rather than large-scale, official strikes, an arrangement that inhibits the former would have its managerial attractions, even if in some circumstances it would increase the effectiveness of the latter.

As Dunn has argued,[17] the hard theory remains largely within the McCarthy framework. The focus remains on the precise functions of the closed shop although some are seen to have been skewed to serve management requirements as well as those of trade unions. The assumption remains that the closed shop has spread because of its significant impact on industrial relations.

THE SOFT THEORY

A closed-shop agreement makes union membership a condition of employment. In itself it does no more than that. It does not, by its mere existence, impel workers to obey union instructions, nor create solidarity, nor eliminate multi-unionism. These functions depend upon the circumstances and timing of the agreement, the ability and motivation of the parties involved to use the closed shop to such ends, and the availability of alternative means to tackle the same problems. So, it would be possible to deny any wider industrial-relations ramifications and suggest that the closed shop has spread merely to incorporate union membership into the individual employment contract. The soft theory builds upon this proposition. Unlike McCarthy, it does not assume that certain effects flow from compulsory union membership. It severs any automatic link between organization and control problems and the appearance of the closed shop to alleviate them, the link that shaped the closed-shop pattern of 1964 and that endures in the hard theory.

To illustrate the difference between the assumptions of the McCarthy analysis and our soft theory, it is worth referring to the Donovan Commission's view of the future of the closed shop. Its report predicted that union interest in the closed shop was likely to diminish as the procedural and institutional reforms it advocated began to permit more unions to organize and bargain without the prop of compulsory membership.[18] That however is only one alternative. If reform had rendered the closed shop's functions superfluous to union needs, then the practice might have withered away. But the soft theory presents a second alternative. It suggests that the result could have been a managerial calculation, upon encountering a union request for a UMA, that its introduction would have little impact upon industrial relations, that the cost of concession would be trifling and that resistance was unnecessary. In other words, the soft theory sees the closed shop's practical functions as having decreased in importance and precisely for that reason offers an explanation of closed-shop growth based on management allowing the practice to flourish as a harmless trade-union foible. To clarify this idea, Dunn has likened the closed shop to the last piece of a jigsaw puzzle which, when assembled, depicts union and management locked into the formal apparatus of joint regulation in industry. The first piece in this jigsaw is the initial union recruitment. The crucial pieces are managerial recognition of union officials and shop stewards as bargaining agents and the conclusion of a comprehensive procedural and substantive agreement. The closed shop is a final piece, a segment of sky or grass that fills the last gap but that, if mislaid, does not significantly detract from the overall effect.[19]

The soft theory requires us to resist the temptation to look for bold patterns of cause and effect. Is it credible, for example, that as the closed shop's major functions became less important, the volume of closed-shop demands became a surge tide? And what of the Warwick Survey's discovery that three-quarters of managers who were familiar with the closed shop saw its advantages?[20] Is it possible to fly in the face of such evidence? Clearly the soft theory needs careful nurturing. Two issues must be considered.

1. If the traditional reasons for unions needing the closed shop do not offer an explanation of contemporary closed-shop growth, are there any residual benefits sufficiently attractive to have provided the impetus behind closed-shop demands? Or can other factors be identified that would have been unlikely to provoke managerial hostility?

2. Is there evidence to suggest that the weakening of managerial resistance to closed-shop demands was not so much a matter of managers finding substantial benefits in the practice, more a judgement that the closed shop would bring few, if any, disadvantages? Can we even explain closed-shop growth in terms of management indifference?

On the union side, we look first at the residual benefits offered by the closed shop, then explore two other factors that might act as additional buttresses supporting the soft theory: the changes in the legal status of the practice in recent years, and its moral and symbolic value to trade unionists:

First, let us look at the residual practical benefits that accrue from union membership becoming a condition of employment. Even if we accept that the chore of recruiting and retaining members has been eased by check-off and by organizers enjoying time off to approach new employees, that union security has been enhanced by sole bargaining rights, and that union influence over the rank and file has been facilitated by the development of shop steward hierarchies and communication networks and a clearer definition of the respective roles of lay and full-time officials – all elements in industrial-relations reform since the mid-1960s – this does not mean that the closed shop offered no attraction to unions. Its contribution to membership stability should not be under-estimated. Nevertheless, beside these reforms, its role would seem peripheral, an indication not of a striving for solidarity and bargaining leverage, but of a book-keeper's desire for neatness and for the last penny of potential revenue. Admittedly such a role might have little emotional appeal for the rank and file. Therefore we would have to argue that the main thrust behind recent closed-shop growth came from those officials and organizers who recognized its usefulness in this specific area. To an extent, such an argument could be supported in that post-1974 UMAs tended not to spring out of unilateral custom and practice attempts to enforce the closed shop. They originated instead in the bargaining machinery and were secured formally by negotiation. Was this an indication of union bureaucracy approaching management bureaucracy with a view to rectifying an administrative untidiness?

A second factor, which Hanson and his colleagues stress, is the 1970s closed-shop legislation. 'The favourable legal climate which TULRA[21] created', they claim, 'must be a major reason for the spread of written UMAs and the growth of the closed shop in the period 1975–80'.[22] The implication of this seems to be that trade unionists were stimulated by the demise of the Industrial Relations Act to press for closed-shop agreements, even if they had no previous interest or need for the practice. Such a suggestion, however, must be treated with caution. Although TULRA heralded a dramatic upsurge in closed-shop demands, the relationship between the two was not so simple. To understand its complexity the law has to be placed in its historical context.

Prior to 1971 the closed shop developed under the protection of the trade-union immunities,[23] and in its own right under the common law relating both to action in defence of trading interests[24] and to the employment contract which permitted the employer to dismiss an employee for any reason, including non-membership of a trade union, without redress.[25] In 1971, however, the Industrial Relations Act placed the closed shop in legal jeopardy by conferring on employees a statutory right not to belong to any union and by declaring pre-entry shops void. Admittedly the law did allow registered trade unions to seek agency shop agreements and approved closed shops, but as most TUC-affiliated unions deregistered as a protest against the legislation, these options were not available to them.[26] Even so, the Act's effect upon existing closed shops proved to be limited. As Weekes and his colleagues showed, the vast majority continued to operate because unions and employers co-operated to discourage individuals from exercising their new right.[27] As regards the spread of the practice, however, the impact of the legislation appears to have been more significant. The late 1960s was a period of increasing closed-shop activity. The 1971 Act halted this activity. Until its repeal by TULRA in 1974, it stood as a breakwater, holding back the tide of closed-shop demands. Its removal released the built-up pressure. Hence the surge of UMAs between 1975 and 1977. But it must be remembered that TULRA did not give trade unions a positive legal right to operate closed shops, nor any legal machinery to secure them. In legal terms it was no easier for a union to obtain a closed shop after 1974 than it had been before 1971. The aim of TULRA, its amendment in 1976, and the Employment Protection Act 1975, all of which impinged upon the closed shop, was to find a *modus vivendi* between compulsory union membership and the unfair dismissal legislation that had been introduced for the first time by the Industrial Relations Act and strengthened by an incoming Labour government pledged to extend individual employment rights. When the law was finalized in 1976 it became automatically fair to dismiss an employee for non-union membership where a UMA was deemed to exist by an industrial tribunal, unless the individual had religious objection to such membership. It was the closest the legislators could come to a return to legal non-intervention in relation to the closed shop which had traditionally prevailed. Thus for Hanson and his colleagues to claim that the favourable legal climate that existed between 1974 and 1980 was a major reason for the growth of the closed shop over the same period is misleading. Closed shops were still a matter of collective bargaining and voluntary agreement. Equally misleading is Hanson *et al.'s* claim that the 1974 change in the law was a contemporary reason for closed-shop growth. It implies that the legal context had never before been so favourable, whereas in fact McCarthy observed the development of the closed shop against a substantially similar legal background. Indeed, Hanson and his colleagues acknowledge this by quoting McCarthy's statement that 'any man may refuse to work with another who is not a member of a specified trade union. . . . Any man, or group of men, may threaten to strike if non-members are not removed. Such acts are legal'.[28] In other words, the legal context is common, if different in detail, to both past and contemporary periods of closed-shop growth.

So, what has been the impact of recent legal changes upon the spread of the closed shop? We see it in negative rather than positive terms. It would be difficult to deny, for example, that the 1971 Act effectively curtailed the closed shop's expansion in the first half of the 1970s. Further it might reasonably be surmised that, had the Act survived until 1980, then the recent growth of closed-shop agreements would not have occurred to anything like the same extent. Similarly, it might be suggested that the 1980 Employment Act, with its provision that new closed shops must be confirmed by 80 per cent of the employees involved to be legally defensible, will make it more difficult for unions to obtain UMAs, although its impact is likely to be less dramatic than the 1971 Act because by 1980 the wave of closed-shop acvitity was almost spent. But if there had been no Industrial Relations Act, no unfair dismissal legislation, no TULRA and no Employment Protection Act, and the closed shop's absentionist legal status had continued uninterrupted throughout the 1970s, then by 1980 the closed-shop population would have been much the same as it actually was in that year.

We now turn to our third argument in support of the soft theory: to what extent were moral values a factor in the recent surge of the closed-shop demands? McCarthy acknowledged that the commonest reason put forward by trade unionists for wanting a closed shop was couched partly in moral terms. Union members claimed to resent 'the continued presence of the non-member, regarding him as a "free rider" who [benfited] from their efforts'.[29] Yet he rejected this as the real reason for closed-shop growth because even where union members had no serious interest in the practice, they nevertheless expressed disapproval of 'free riders'. It seemed to be a sentiment almost universal among trade unionists. He argued instead that there needed to be deeper, more practical reasons, such as recruitment difficulties, a breakaway union, or the need for strike discipline, to galvanize the union into mounting a closed-shop campaign with enough vigour to break employer opposition[30]. Here we contend that this argument no longer held true in the post- McCarthy period. As practical considerations became less significant and management attitudes made closed shops easier to achieve, moral factors assumed a greater importance. The idea that non-unionism was morally wrong could be accepted at face value as a reason for the closed shop's spread. Indeed it provided the element of popular support for its growth so far lacking in our soft theory.

What evidence is there of such popular support? According to Hanson and his colleagues, public opinion polls carried out in 1959 and 1979 indicate that as the closed shop spread, its popularity declined.[31] In 1959 Gallup found that 70 per cent of union members felt that unionists were justified in putting pressure upon non-members to join the union by refusing to work with them, whereas in 1979 Opinion Research Centre found that only 12 per cent of members agreed that those who refuse to join a union for moral, political or other strong reasons should be sacked. The trend appears obvious. Yet it cannot be accepted uncritically. Are Hanson and his colleagues comparing like with like? The 1959 and 1979 questions are framed very differently. The first, which avoids mention of the sack and which in full refers to a workplace where the majority are in the union and the minority are a source of weakness in wage negotiations, might be expected to have elicited responses rather more favourable to the closed shop than the second, which implies that compulsory membership rides roughshod over certain strongly held principles. Consequently, the two questions are a dubious indication of an historical trend.

To be fair to Hanson and his colleagues they do quote other, less decisive results from the 1979 survey.[32] Yet these merely emphasize both the dangers of casual comparisons and the complexity of trade unionists' attitudes towards the closed shop. Certainly, questions that mentioned dismissal in connection with the closed shop stimulated a high degree of hostility to the practice. But, for example, a question that referred to non-members being made to join the union' attracted a less hostile response. Indeed, a majority of trade unionists (54 per cent) agreed that 'all people working for large companies should be made to join the union if a vote is taken and a majority of workers want a . . . closed shop arrangement'. Considering that this 54 per cent exceeded the proportion of union members then in closed shops, the response can be interpreted as substantial support among trade unionists for compulsory membership. Even if they were more squeamish about seeing people sacked their opinions were not necessarily inconsistent. For instance, the findings may indicate that many union members supported closed-shop demands because they considered that non-members' meanness in avoiding union dues did not run sufficiently deep for them to prefer the sack to parting with their money and that therefore a closed-shop agreement would be effective in making them join. Moreover, many contemporary UMAs were not absolute in compelling membership, allowing dispensations that might have been expected to counteract some of the doubts of ordinary union members.

Thus, carefully read, the opinion polls do not conclusively show that the closed shop has become an anathema to trade unionists. Nor, admittedly, do they show overwhelming or even clear-cut approval. Rather they suggest that, although union members' views on the subject are complex and sometimes ambivalent, there is a degree of accord with some of the intentions behind such arrangements, linked particularly with a moral rejection of the 'free rider' and a belief that everybody should be in the union if the majority wishes it. This adds a popular dimensions, based on group values, to our soft theory of closed-shop growth.

It is possible moreover to push this line of reasoning further, albeit on a narrower front. If trade unionists' attitudes were analysed in further detail, we might expect the strongest feelings in favour of the closed shop to come from the minority of committed trade unionists, including full-time officials, lay activists, and particularly shop stewards. These would have been the people who formulated closed-shop demands in recent years and pressed their claims upon management. These would also have been the people most aware of trade-union principles and the historical bases for them. Such traditionally closed industries as coal-mining, dockworking, printing, shipbuilding and heavy engineering have a special significance in trade-union history from which the closed shop cannot be divorced. Because of the often bitter conflict that took place in these industries, the unions involved have come to epitomize worker solidarity. Could we therefore argue that committed trade unionists elsewhere started to associated such solidarity with the closed shops that accompanied it? Has the closed shop become its symbol? If we accept the importance of folklore to such activists, then we could plausibly surmise that the closed shop means far more to them than an administrative convenience to secure and sustain 100 per cent membership or to prise subscriptions from 'free riders'. We might say that committed trade unionists had a 'gut feeling' about the closed shop: especially in areas where traditions of strong trade unionism had not previously existed or in areas where well-organized but open unions had long existed but where reform had given shop stewards far more autonomy and responsibility than in the past. For such activists the negotiation of a closed shop may have acted as a kind of rite of passage, a ritual endorsement of the collective values of the trade-union movement, a confirmation of the status and legitimacy of their new role, and a mark of their emergence into the world of collective bargaining. It alluded, perhaps unspokenly, to past struggles in what are now the heartlands of strong trade unionism. It allowed inexperienced shop stewards to compare themselves with trade unionists of longer pedigree – the miners, the dockers and the compositors. To sum up, whereas McCarthy treated the closed shop as a practical instrument to achieve solidarity, here it is treated as an *expression* of solidarity, a solidarity that might or might not exist.[33] According to our soft theory, this, together with certain administrative advantages to union organizers, and popular feelings against non-members as 'free riders', provided the impetus behind latter-day closed-shop growth.

Turning to the management side, the argument here is that management became more willing to concede closed-shop agreements in the latter twenty years because the practice became increasingly peripheral to industrial relations. Over this period a management strategy that became increasingly common was to encourage order and stability in the workplace through greater union security. The hard theory saw the closed shop as an important component in this security. By constrast, the soft theory suggests that the crucial factors in securing the union's position in the firm were such arrangements as recognition of shop steward commitees, time off for union duties, sole bargaining rights and check-off. Beside these the closed shop was a marginal factor. But because it did not contradict the thinking behind their strategy, managers allowed the practice to appear almost as a by-product of such reforms to satisfy certain trade-union needs that were considered harmless to the company. For example, if the closed shop alleviated some of the chore of maintaining membership, that was likely neither to appear damaging to management, nor to offer them substantial benefits. Equally, if the closed shop had symbolic importance for union activists, that might not even have been recognized by management or at least have been judged to carry no practical significance.

In developing this proposition, it would be insufficient to quote the Warwick survey's findings that of those managers with experience of the closed shop half saw no disadvantages in it.[34] This would merely throw into sharper relief the fact that three-quarters of the same sample reported advantages. So the immediate task is to reconcile the reported managerial praise of the closed shop with our indifference thesis. First, we might suggest that managers tended to exaggerate the virtues of the closed shop, partly to justify their toleration of a controversial practice, partly to give the impression that their company had a coherent policy on the matter, and partly, in the case of industrial-relations specialists, to show they were aware of the textbook benefits.[35] Second, the kind of survey commissioned by the Warwick researchers tends to lose shades of opinion in aggregated results. In other words, it was not that managers overpraised the closed shop, but that tentative judgements of slight or potential advantages were combined with perceived major advantages to produce a broad category of positive attitudes. Third, it is important to distinguish between management attitudes towards the closed shop as part of the *status quo* and the reasons why such arrangements were conceded to the unions in the first place. A manager might have agreed to a closed shop when, say, 99 per cent of manual workers were in the union because at such a density it was immaterial to the company whether the union had a closed shop or not. Yet, when subsequently faced with a questionnaire, the same manager could have said without inconsistency that the closed shop was beneficial in preventing multi-unionism. His answer would have been valid in so far as the practice does by its nature shut the door more tightly against encroaching unions than does 99 per cent voluntary membership, even though that was not a significant factor in ushering the agreement in.

Pursuing this point, an indication of whether or not management conceded the closed shop to prevent multi-unionism would be the membership density guidelines applied when considering demands for the practice. The more cautious these guidelines were, that is, the nearer membership had to be to 100 per cent before management was willing to concede a closed shop, the more likely the company had already been saddled with multi-unionism or had avoided it. In short, if managers tended to acquiesce to closed-shop agreements only when the bulk of the workforce was recruited by voluntary means and the union/s were securely bound into joint institutions, then it would be difficult to argue that they used the practice as a tactical weapon to prevent multi-unionism. We would have to conclude that they only began to treat closed-shop demands sympathetically when its introduction meant little more than the mopping up of the last pockets of non-unionism. To the union this may have been useful. To management, it was likely to have been of little significance.

We turn now to the closed shop's discipline function, a function that in theory can work for or against managerial interests. Here we must sustain the argument that in neither direction was this an, important factor when management considered closed-shop demands. Support stems from the fact that, although much industrial-relations research has focused on industrial conflict and such facets of union indiscipline as unofficial and unconstitutional strikes, it is remarkable how seldom the closed shop is mentioned in the academic literature. Batstone *et al*'s analysis of how shop steward leaders exercise their authority over the remainder of the stewards and the membership in a large factory offers a particularly pertinent example.[36] Although a closed shop operated throughout the manual grades involved, it received no mention as a weapon to control the shop-floor. Instead the convenors and a 'quasi-elite' of senior stewards exercised 'great power'[37] over the workforce through a wide and complex network of formal and informal relationships. Sectionalism was not eliminated and custom and practice flourished despite the factory agreement. Yet 'populist stewards', who tended to champion sectional causes and around whom discontented groups might have coalesced, suffered the worst of two worlds. Not only were they unable to penetrate the steward hierarchy that monopolized the formal rule-making process, but ironically they were also less capable of furthering sectional interests than those stewards identified with the 'quasi-elite'. Precisely because they were starved of resources and contacts, including those within management, and precisely because they played little part in the formulation of the factory agreement, populists tended to be less adept than leader stewards at manipulating the system to the benefit of their immediate work groups. In short, the various institutional and social networks of the leader stewards ensured their domination of both the informal and the formal industrial relations of the plant without recourse to use of the closed shop as a punitive instrument. If Batsone *et al.*'s study was at all typical, it might be concluded that any manager assessing a closed-shop demand and seeking guidance from either existing closed shops within the company or from the way shop steward authority worked generally, would have found it difficult to sustain the view that the introduction of a UMA would be likely to have a major impact on union discipline. Such discipline was maintained by other means.

There remains one further aspect of the closed shop that would have seemed a potential barrier to management indifference. Traditionally employers found it distasteful to force unwilling employees into union membership, and while it could be imagined that the possibility of substantial benefits would have been sufficient for management to swallow moral objections to the practice, an absence of benefits might not. Even though it has been said that managers in large companies, 'reared in a collectivist ethos, have little or no sympathy with the "free rider" who takes the benefits of union membership without paying the dues',[38] there is a distinction between lack of sympathy with 'free riders' and a willingness to see them dismissed. To an extent, the dilemma seems to have been resolved by the UMA formula, under which non-members already employed when the closed shop was introduced and those with specific objections to trade unionism were not compelled to join the union.[39] Such exemptions, backed by formal procedures to deal with individual problems, suggest a degree of compromise between union and management in keeping with our soft theory. Union negotiators have been willing to settle for ensuring that those already in the union stay in and that new employees automatically join. They have accepted that 100 per cent membership must wait upon labour turnover and the recruitment of existing non-members by methods used in an open shop.

To sum up, the soft theory states that the post-entry closed shop spread in the period mid-1960s to 1980 because it became a lower key issue than it formerly was. Reforms, especially at workplace level, rendered the closed shop less vital to union effectiveness. Minor benefits offered by the practice, however, together with its symbolic value to committed trade unionists and a degree of rank and file antipathy towards 'free riders', sustained union interest in the closed shop. Previously, management resistance would have contained much of this pressure. But, recognizing in recent years that the closed shop was unlikely to have much effect upon their industrial relations, managers increasingly looked upon closed-shop demands with some dispassion and, because unions pursued their claims with limited vigour, were able to negotiate liberal UMAs, which did not force them into disagreeable confrontations with non-members. In a sentence, weak closed-shop demands met with weak resistance and resulted in diluted closed-shop arrangements which performed marginal functions.

5 The Growth of the Post-entry Closed Shop since the mid-1960s: Explanations

To test the two theories of closed-shop growth we divided the British economy into three: nationalized industries, local authorities and private-sector manufacturing.

THE NATIONALIZED INDUSTRIES

By the end of the 1970s three-quarters of employees in the nationalized industries were covered by closed-shop arrangements. This was approximately a quarter of the entire closed-shop population. As the bulk of these arrangements have appeared since the late 1960s, the nationalized sector would seem a crucial testing ground for our theories.

At the beginning of the 1960s the nationalized industries were just as crucial to McCarthy's theory. The limited extent of the closed shop there indicated that heavily unionized areas were not necessarily fertile ground for closed-shop growth. He suggested that trade unionists in public corporations had little interest in the closed shop because they felt no practical need for it. Encouraged by the statutory obligations upon management to recognize, consult and bargain with them, unions had flourished in a stable industrial-relations environment, enjoying a high degree of security and achieving a high level of membership without the aid of the closed shop. Moreover, the apparent moratorium on official use of the strike weapon in the years following nationalization in the late 1940s meant that any weakness in solidarity caused by non-unionists remained latent. Certainly there was no great pressure upon the unions to negotiate formal closed-shop agreements through the national bargaining machinery. Nor did rumbling complaints from within the unions about 'free riders' shake management's resolve to resist the

57

imposition of compulsory union membership. The 'Treasury view' was that the principles of Whitleyism presupposed voluntary trade unionism and, while the Treasury was only responsible for industrial relations in the Civil Service, including at that time the Post Office, this stance spilled over into the nationalized sector.[1]

Some closed shops did exist however. But again these merely confirmed McCarthy's theory. Some had been inherited upon nationalization. The informal closed shop among coal-miners, for example, which according to McCarthy had grown out of the need for strike solidarity over a long period,[2] continued when the industry was taken into public ownership. Similarly, closed shops had tended to develop in craft areas, such as the railway workshops, or where a corporation was involved in a closed-shop sector, as in the docks where the nationalized concerns followed the Dockwork Regulation Scheme of 1946. Only rarely had closed shops appeared subsequent to nationalization. In London Transport, for instance, a breakaway, the National Transport Workers' Union, prompted management to agree under duress to a T&GWU closed shop for busmen in 1946 to eliminate its competitor.[3] In the nationalised airlines, on the other hand, management avoided formal recognition of the closed shop by adopting a system of '100 per cent Notifications,' under which it was agreed that no non-unionists would be introduced into areas where union membership was universal among the existing workforce.

As McCarthy completed his study, the closed-shop issue was beginning to stir within the nationalized industries. Activity became more intense towards the end of the 1960s. It culminated in a flurry of UMAs between 1969 and 1971, a lull during the period of the Industrial Relations Act (1971–4), then a second, greater burst of activity in 1974–8. The chronology below indicates its extent:

1969:	Electricity Supply Industry	– UMA for manuals
	BEA/BOAC (later British Airways)	– UMA for pilots
1970:	British Rail	– UMAs for manuals and non-manuals
	National Freight (BRS side)	– UMA for manuals
	London Transport	– UMA for railway manuals and non-manuals

1971:	National Freight (NC/F side)	– UMA for manuals
1973:	National Coal Board	– agency shop agreement for management grades
1974:	British Rail	– UMAs reactivated after repeal of Industrial Relations Act and further groups added – six UMAs in all
1975:	British Gas	– UMA for manuals
	National Coal Board	– UMA for non-manuals
1976:	British Airways	– six UMAs (one reactivated) for manuals and non-manuals
	British Rail	– amendment of 1974 UMAs in light of TULR(A)A.
	London Transport	– four UMAs either reactivating or formalizing previous arrangements or establishing new closed shop for manuals and non-manuals.
	National Freight	– amendment of 1970–1 UMAs in light of TULR(A)A
	British Gas	– UMA for non-manual
	Post Office	– two UMAs for manuals and non-manuals
	National Bus	– UMA for manuals – enabling agreement for local implementation
	National Water Council	– UMA for manual grades
1977:	Electricity Supply Industry	– UMA for non-manuals
	London Transport	– UMAs extending closed shop into four more grades
	British Shipbuilders	– closed shop for manuals formalized in national agreement
	British Steel	UMA for manuals and non-manuals – enabling agreement for local implementation
	National Water Council	– UMA for craft grades

1978:	London Transport	– UMA covering one further grade
	British Transport	
	Docks	– four UMAs accepted in principle for manual and non-manuals; not signed because of unresolved inter-union dispute but operates in spirit

This chronology is important to our analysis. The spread of the closed shop in the nationalized industries can be seen as a single movement, rather than a series of discrete actions. The timing of individual agreements and the resultant cross-fertilization that occurred within particular corporations and between them is a key element within this movement. It can be broadly divided into two phases. In the initial phase (1960–71) the long germination period, which produced the first crop of nationally negotiated UMAs, tends to offer evidence in support of our 'hard theory'. In the secondary phase (1974–8) during which such UMAs became commonplace, our 'soft theory' would seem more appropriate an explanation of the closed shop's growth.

The Initial Phase (1960–71)

Having said that closed-shop activity in the nationalized industries during the 1960s conforms with our hard theory, it is necessary to hedge that statement with the comment that isolating the principal reasons for such activity is not easy. For example, trade union records on their closed-shop demands tended to offer a variety of arguments in support of the practice. This was especially true of conference debates where delegates were intent upon building a cast-iron case in its favour. Moreover, the process of converting these arguments into a case to convince management of the efficacy of a UMA meant further modification.

Nevertheless, in the 1960s there emerged conditions that, according to the hard theory, made the nationalized industries ripe for closed-shop demands. They might be described as the beginnings of disillusionment: a realization among the unions and their members that employment in the nationalized sector was no more comfortable and sometimes less so than employment in the private sector. The issues involved were pay, efficiency, and technical and organizational change. To illustrate them we have chosen British Rail, because the railway unions were in the vanguard of the closed-shop movement and their spheres of influence covered other public corporations which showed closed-shop activity, such as London Transport, the National Freight Corporation, the British Transport Docks Board and the National Bus Company.

In practice it is difficult to separate these various issues. By starting with the pay question, it is possible to see how they intertwined. Initially trouble arose over whether wage levels should be determined by comparability criteria or by the ability of the corporation concerned to pay. Almost immediately productivity factors were added to the equation and shortly afterwards incomes policy norms provided a further complication. As early as 1955 the Cameron Inquiry noted that the British Transport Commission (BTC) was unable to offer railway-men the level of pay it wished because the 1947 Transport Act placed upon it the responsibility of making the rail system pay its way. But Cameron also felt that rail employees should receive a fair and adequate wage and be no worse off than workers in comparable industries.[4] The 1955 dispute was only settled by a seventeen-day official strike by ASLEF members – the first on such a scale in the nationalized industries – and a further Court of Inquiry. Even so, the pay issue continued to fester. Against a background of increasing discontent, with the NUR, whose members had not received a pay increase in the two years after 1958, threatening a strike, the Guillebaud Committee undertook a large-scale comparability study the findings of which guided the rail unions in their pay demands throughout the 1960s. Under pressure from the government, which was keen both to curb railway spending and to moderate public-sector wage rises, the manage-ment side was less enthusiastic. Already committed to a rationalization of the railway network, it made efforts to woo the unions away from the comparability principle towards criteria based on efficiency.

This rationalization programme had begun in the mid-1950s. Until then the railways had changed little since Victorian times. The railway map was much the same as at the turn of the century, locomotives were still steam driven and even the timetables had endured. Methods of signalling and permanent way maintenance, and of marshalling and sorting goods wagons had altered little. After cautious beginnings, the process of change accelerated after 1963 with the Beeching Plan to the extent that by the end of the decade the railways were transformed. In 1960, for instance, 14 500 steam-engines provided traction. By 1969 these had been replaced by a mere 4500 diesel and electric locomotives. Over the same period, power signalling reduced the number of signal boxes from some 9000 to 5000 while marshalling yards were reduced from 878 to 184 and the number of stations from 7500 to 3200. In addition, thirteen out of twenty-nine workshops were closed. The workforce meanwhile diminished from 518 000 to 296 000.[5] All this was not achieved without conflict. In 1962, for example, 270 000 workers participated in an official one-day strike as a protest against the closure of branch lines and workshops, while between 1964 and 1967 there were various works to rule and other unofficial actions over productivity bonuses and new working arrangements. Indeed, two further Courts of Inquiry were convened to investigate particularly intractable problems.[6] Moreover, in 1966 a National Board for Prices and Incomes report[7] expressed doubts about the continued validity of the Guillebaud comparisons and supported a closer integration between pay and productivity. Its recommendations were rejected by the NUR whose threatened strike was only called off after prime ministerial intervention stressed the importance of productivity criteria in wage bargaining as encouraged by the existing incomes policy. Despite the unions' continued faith in Guillebaud, the first stage of a comprehensive pay and efficiency agreement, in line with incomes policy, was concluded in 1968 and a second stage introduced in 1969. It was as part of this second package that trade-union membership became a condition of employment in the relevant grades from January 1970.[8]

The experience of the rail unions was repeated to some extent in the other nationalized industries where closed-shop demands moved towards fruition in the late 1960s. For example, although in a far healthier financial position than the railways, the electricity supply industry coupled the closure of old, labour-intensive power-stations and the introduction of large generating units with a series of productivity agreements between 1964 and 1968 which reduced systematic overtime, increased labour flexibility and brought in incentive payments based on work study, a technique previously little used. According to Pryke, the *sine qua non* of the success of these reforms was the co-operative attitude of the electricity unions which 'mounted a determined campaign to persuade their reluctant rank and file to accept the agreements'.[9] In the nationalized airlines between 1967 and 1969 a dispute over pay and productivity led to the British Airline Pilots' Association withdrawal temporarily from the National Joint Council for Civil Air Transport, two Courts of Inquiry and two strikes.[10] Perhaps closest to the railway experience was that of the Post Office. As part of the Civil Service until 1969, the Post Office was influenced by the principle of fair comparisons, as affirmed by the Priestley Commission in 1956. The 1961 public-sector pay pause undermined this principle and the former UPW (now the Union of Communication Workers) responded with a work to rule and overtime ban. The situation was exacerbated by subsequent pay norms. By 1964 the union estimated that a 20 per cent rise was needed to re-establish the differentials that had existed in 1956. Despite a Committee of Inquiry, a one-day strike was called in 1964. Meanwhile financial difficulties impelled Post Office management towards securing greater efficiency. Management consultants were called in during 1965 and reported that a substantial proportion of postmen's time was spent unproductively. This stimulated a long period of productivity bargaining intended to alter established patterns of sorting and delivery. As these had sustained levels of overtime in low-paid jobs, the changes were treated with suspicion by employees.[11]

Together these examples indicate the heightening tensions within the nationalized sector during the 1960s. According to our hard theory, they provide suitable conditions for the emergence of closed-shop demands. Indeed they would seem to epitomize its ambivalent nature. On the one hand, discontent over pay, resistance to efficiency drives, and in some cases a decrease in job security provided a popular basis for increased militancy and hence increased interest in the closed shop as the actual or potential menace of non-unionists became apparent. On the other, the union leadership, enmeshed with varying degrees of enthusiasm in the complexities of productivity bargaining, encountered membership opposition against which the closed shop would have been a useful disciplinary weapon, at least preventing the disaffected from 'voting with their feet' by resigning, joining another union or setting up a breakaway organization. How far did the timing and articulation of the closed-shop demands conform to this thesis?

Initially, a number of coincidences can be pointed out. For example, the UPW conference passed its first motion in favour of the closed shop in 1964 during the pay dispute that prompted a one-day strike and a work to rule. On the railways, a similar proposition had been adopted rather earlier – in 1939 – by the NUR. As the general union in the industry its interest reflected the problems of organizing a wide range of grades in a scattered workforce. Little progress was made in the face of management opposition, however, until ASLEF and TSSA were willing to support the principle. Their attitude only changed at the beginning of the 1960s, once conflict over pay, modernization and rationalization began to simmer. ASLEF, which had long enjoyed high and stable levels of membership among footplatemen and had enjoyed a craft solidarity which made a closed shop unnecessary, passed its first pro-closed shop resolution in 1960 as the phasing out of steam threatened traditional skills. The white-collar TSSA reversed a conference decision of the previous year and adopted a closed-shop policy in 1963 when the Beeching cuts were known. It seems that in all three unions the agitation came from local activists rather than the national officials. For instance, in 1965 the General Secretary of the NUR, Sidney Greene, spoke against an AGM closed-shop proposition, claiming that the introduction of check-off in that year had effectively set the railway industry on the road towards union membership as a condition of service. The fact that the proposition was nevertheless carried decisively indicated the importance of the closed shop to the committed rank and file.[12] Sidney Greene acknowledged this the following year in his evidence to the Donovan Commission: '. . . . If everybody benefits from the trade union activity . . . they should make a contribution to it as well. . . . It does not worry me. But it used to worry me when I worked on the railway.'[13] These comments endorsed the NUR's written evidence which observed that local action was often taken by its members to persuade non-members into the union, sometimes to the extent of unofficial strikes.[14]

It is important to specify why such 'free rider' arguments belong to the hard rather than the soft theory. The latter says that resentment of 'free riders' can be translated into background support for a closed-shop claim in circumstances where the issue is low key and management requires little propulsion into an agreement. In this case, by contrast, we are suggesting that such resentment fluctuates over time. Periods of trauma and conflict, as in the nationalized industries during the 1960s, heighten it by revealing non-members' lack of participation in union activities, and by pointing to the wider practical implications of the closed shop. This provides a driving force sufficient to convince an obdurate employer that the closed-shop demand is serious. In the Post Office, for instance, the resurgence of UPW interest in compulsory membership, demonstrated by the castigation of 'free riders' by several delegates at the 1969 conference, coincided with a second work to rule and one-day strike. Of course, it is difficult to ascertain the extent of such feelings when the claim covers a wide variety of localities and jobs. Yet even in a branch where, according to Moran's Colchester survey in 1969, 85 per cent of the membership were opposed to a closed shop, as many as 55 per cent supported the idea of some kind of sanctions against strike breakers.[15] Elsewhere in the UPW attitudes towards the closed shop itself were more positive. Certainly the union appeared confident of mass support. In its formal claim presented to management in 1969, it stressed that there was 'a determination on the part of the vast majority of the members to enforce this demand by a refusal to work with non-union labour'.[16] Nor was the UPW alone in adopting a militant stance in pursuit of the closed shop. As a prelude to securing such as agreement in 1969, BALPA members went into dispute with BOAC over the employment of non-union pilots,[17] while in the National Freight Corporation, the manual unions made it clear to management that their members would strike over the issue if the 1971–2 agreements were not conceded.[18]

It would appear, therefore, that the catalyst involved in the upsurge of closed-shop demands was the industrial unrest in the nationalized sector during the 1960s. It built up the pressure from below which impelled union officials to pursue the issue with vigour. We would not necessarily suggest that this was an exact match with the hard theory. After all, the unions were generally well organized, non-members were few, and participation in industrial action was good. So there was an element of soft-theory ritual present. Encountering managerial productivity initiatives and unable to secure equitable pay settlements, the rank and file, and particularly local activists, responded by expressing their hostility and declaring their solidarity through the medium of closed-shop agitation, even if in practical terms it offered no remedy to their difficulties. Nevertheless, the circumstances suggest a tendency towards the hard rather than the soft theory, especially when we consider that as the decade wore on closed-shop claims began to be articulated in a rather different way.

The change represented a synthesis of union officials' and management thinking. Well into the decade management in the industries under consideration continued to express their traditional aversion to the closed shop. At the 1965 NUR Conference, Sidney Greene assured delegates that management would never agree to compulsory union membership.[19] In the same year, the Postmaster-General rejected the UPWs first application for a closed shop,[20] and three years later the National Freight Corporation treated a claim from its clerical unions in the same manner. Yet a shift in management attitudes could be detected in the mid-1960s. The London Transport Board publicly acknowledged 'considerable advantages in just having one organisation to deal with and having all the men concerned in membership of the trade union'.[21] In the same forum, during discussion of the penalties that might be imposed upon unofficial strikers, the British Railways Board chairman stated: 'If we are going to modernise the trade union structure and re-define its function . . . and we are going to have sanctions that everybody agreed would be applied in the event of unofficial action . . . I would be prepared to consider the implications of that from the point of view of 100 per cent union membership.'[22] The more management drew union officials into the labyrinth of productivity bargaining, the more this argument came to be appreciated. The cost to the unions' leadership of participating in efficiency exercises was high in terms of membership loss, where manpower cuts were involved, and employee disaffection. One facet of this disaffection was the increased aggression of a number of splinter unions. Membership retention had been a continuing problem for the ETU, the main manual union in the CEGB, and the position was exacerbated as the centre of generation moved from London, where ETU loyalty had been strong, to the new power-stations in the north. Here the Electricity Supply Union made progress behind the banner of one specialist union for the industry. The Post Office's breakaway union had a longer pedigree. By 1969 the National Guild of Telephonists had secured 10 000 members among male telephonists, where the UPW was the minority union with a density of about 34 per cent in contrast to a coverage of in excess of 90 per cent elsewhere.[23] A similar sectional union existed on the railways – the Union of Railway Signalmen – which gained from the discontent expressed by signalmen at the 1968–9 pay and efficiency proposals.[24]

It is important not to exaggerate the impact of these breakaway organizations. Yet their existence underlined the difficulties involved in imposing union discipline where members could register their protests by opting out of membership. Realizing it allowed management and union to find common ground on the hitherto contentious closed-shop issue, a point that the unions were not slow to exploit. The UPW's claim argued that with the advent of productivity bargaining in 1968 the efficient development of the Post Office had become intertwined in the efforts of the union to improve the real standard of living of its members. This, the union contended:

> has led to a situation in which the UPW may agree to an increase in pay and in return pledges that UPW members will where necessary accept that they should undertake a number of specified changes in working practices. From the point of view of management it is obviously essential that the union should be able to give and honour such a pledge, and the union in turn can only feel able to give such a pledge if it feels able to persuade, or in very exceptional circumstances compel, its members to accept the changed working practices which the pay increase in question is related to.[25]

The dilemma was echoed from the management side in the British Railways Board statement that 'the prime object of the [closed shop] agreements was to enable the trade unions to have more control over their members in dealing with industrial action not officially supported by the union(s) concerned'.[26] To ensure that this was clearly understood, the Board secured from the rail unions a clause within their UMA, the bare bones of which was: 'In the event of any members of the staff participating in any form of unconstitutional action . . . the Trade Unions shall not afford them any support . . . and may consider taking disciplinary action' (Clause 8).

So, a flurry of what in the mid-1970s came to be known as corporatist sentiments ushered in the first batch of large-scale closed-shop agreements. Demands that had been initiated and sustained by rank and file agitation reached fruition as part of the search for greater control over that rank and file. The sound that accompanied these ironic developments was of dominoes falling. The nationalized industry managements watched each other carefully, each reluctant to be first to take a step, the consequences of which were unknown and potentially unpopular with political masters and public opinion. But once the electricity supply industry had shown the way, BOAC, the over- and underground railways and the National Freight Corporation quickly followed suit. In the Post Office a closed shop was agreed in principle and in the gas industry and the British Transport Docks Board negotiations were well advanced when the 1971 Industrial Relations Act interceded. Both the UPW and the gas manual unions had to wait until the mid-1970s to secure their UMAs.

The Secondary Phase (1974–8)

Our soft theory offers a better explanation of the secondary phase of closed-shop growth in the nationalized industrialized industries than the hard theory applied to the initial phase. Again this was a tendency rather than a polarization. The shift occurred not because industrial relations became less combative than in the 1960s, but because the pioneering negotiations of the late 1960s established the closed shop as an accepted feature of public corporation employment. In the two years following the repeal of the Industrial Relations Act[27] this impression was reinforced by the largely non-contentious discussions aimed at reviving and modifying the UMAs that had existed prior to the Act. Together with the completion of the interrupted negotiations in British Gas and the Post Office, these promoted the idea that the closed shop was no longer an issue between management and unions. Hence managers and union officials interviewed commonly attributed the emergence of

UMAs during this period to a general change in attitudes towards the practice rather than to reasons specific to their own organization.

For management two factors were important in dealing with a closed-shop claim. First, managers knew that if they conceded a UMA they would not be the first and they would not be alone. Unlike the corporations that faced closed-shop pressure in the 1960s, they were not diverging from a long-held principle, nor were they taking a step into the unknown. Second, they could learn from the experiences of their predecessors. For example, the Electricity Supply UMA's exemption of existing non-unionists set the pattern for minimizing conflict between the closed shop and personal liberty and became standard in the typical UMAs newly established after 1974. British Rail provided a warning of what might happen if such a dispensation were not adopted. It progressively tightened its closed-shop agreement until by 1976 only religious exemptions were allowed. As a result, some forty employees were dismissed by the end of 1977 for failing to join the union.[28] To avoid such problems a number of corporations, notably British Airways, took the initiative once their unions had expressed an interest in the closed shop and tried to prevent union attitudes hardening towards non-members by making it clear that management had no objection to compulsory union membership and would not delay its introduction provided a suitably liberal agreement could be reached.[29] Indeed, exemptions and procedures to deal with them tended to provide the focus of discussion rather than any industrial-relations implications. Management appeared to accept the logic of compulsory membership where union density was high. The costs involved were calculated to be minor. Even expectations of advantages were less pronounced than in the late 1960s. Whereas at that time corporatist arguments relating to workforce discipline played a prominent part in managerial thinking, in the secondary phase such hopes were more muted. Managers interviewed during 1978, when closed-shop negotiations were still fresh in their minds, spoke of 'regularizing the union membership position', of 'tidying up industrial-relations procedures', and of 'converting long standing high levels of union membership into a formal UMA'.[30] Such comments conform with our soft theory. The introduction of the closed shop was an institutional adjustment, not a dramatic step.

Given that management was inclined to see no significant costs in conceding the practice, what was the incentive for unions to pursue closed-shop claims in the second half of the 1970s? Of general significance, the shift in managerial attitudes had made the closed shop accessible – a realistic, even easy, target. No longer was it a holy grail, to be lengthily and arduously sought without guarantee of success. It was there for the taking, irrespective of a union's practical needs or of the reasons presented for wanting it. Not to exploit the opportunity might have been seen as a weakness, an admission that the union lacked the solidarity that the closed shop expressed. In the case of NALGO (Electricity Supply and British Gas), the CPSA (Post Office) and other white-collar unions such feelings appear to have been particularly important. Taking NALGO as our example, the union had been gradually changing in character from the archetypal cautious, co-operative Whitley trade union, in which chief officers, who wore both union and management hats, enjoyed considerable influence, to a more aggressive body in which a left-wing 'action group' reflected a new militant mood among its activists. A landmark in this change was NALGO's affiliation to the TUC in 1964 which, according to Undy *et al.*, 'brought with it a package of general attitudes that would have appeared alien to NALGO in the past. These influenced the development of unionate concepts such as showing solidarity and refusing to black-leg during other unions' disputes'.[31] The closed shop might also be included as a 'unionate concept'. For NALGO activists it symbolized the union's new attitude towards industrial relations. It put NALGO on an equal footing with the manual unions in the gas and electricity supply industries which had recently secured closed-shop agreements. It was, to quote the previous chapter, a ritual endorsement of the collective values of the trade-union movement and a mark of the union's emergence into the world of collective bargaining. This argument also has a wider relevance. It can be applied to certain manual unions such as the GMWU in the water supply industry, then one of the less solidaristic segments of the union. In following the GMWU sections in Electricity Supply and Gas down the closed-shop road in 1976, it could claim parity with them at least on that issue.

It would, however, be misleading to suggest that there were no practical benefits on offer to the unions that sought closed shops after 1974. The GMWU in the water industry secured a relatively tight agreement, exempting only conscientious and religious objectors, and because union density was 70 per cent when the UMA was signed, membership gains were achieved. Yet this is very much the exception that proves the rule. Elsewhere, the lesser administrative advantage of stabilizing existing membership was bought at the cost of allowing existing non-members to remain outside the unions concerned. As for the possibility of increasing strike solidarity, it is significant that union officials interviewed did not regard this as a major factor in the closed-shop campaign. At the time, such officials were involved in the 'Social Contract' between the trade-union movement and the Labour government. By offering wage restraint in return for economic, industrial and social reform the unions held in abeyance the kind of mass industrial action that had punctuated the years of the previous Conservative administration. Consequently, in the immediate circumstances of the post-1974 closed-shop demands the need for strike solidarity was less pressing. On the other hand, it could be argued that during this 'corporatist' period, the closed shop's discipline function would have helped union officials 'deliver the membership' and thus their side of the Contract. Yet officials interviewed echoed the management opinion that controlling dissidents was not uppermost in negotiators'minds, a view reinforced by the fact that the instigators of closed-shop demands tended to be the rank and file activists who would have also provided the core of dissent against the prevailing wage restraint policy. In fact it could be argued that the closed-shop issue helped fill the gap in the negotiating agenda left by the unions' voluntary suspension of free collective bargaining over pay. A successful closed-shop campaign might have acted as a placebo to soothe discontented activists.

THE LOCAL AUTHORITIES

The origins of the recent spate of closed-shop demands in local authorities can also be traced back to the 1960s, although the major growth period occurred after 1974 and lasted until 1979 and 1980 when a flurry of UMAs added 20 per cent to the closed-shop population in local government.[32] Closed-shop penetration was nevertheless more restricted than in the nationalized sector. By 1980 about half a million local authority employees were covered by some kind of closed-shop arrangements and, while this was a huge increase on McCarthy's 45 000 estimate in the early 1960s, it represented only 20 per cent of the workforce. Even among manual workers little more than a third were involved although this amounted to over 85 per cent of the closed-shop population. Less than one in three of firemen were similarly covered. Of the two large white-collar bargaining units, the closed shop extended to only 10 per cent of administrative, professional, technical and clerical employees and to no teachers. In general closed shops were found in the major conurbations. For example, in England and Wales 85 per cent of the closed-shop population was concentrated in metropolitan counties and districts and the various London authorities. Following the national pattern, the new closed shops have almost invariably been post-entry in character. This type encompassed 87 per cent of those in closed shops. The remaining 13 per cent were skilled manual workers covered by informal pre-entry arrangements which were tacitly accepted by management. Apart from these, the trend has been towards greater formality. By the end of the 1970s nearly two-thirds of the closed-shop population fell within the jurisdiction of written UMAs.

McCarthy's explanation for the existence of the closed shop in local government departed from the main thrust of his theory. 'Where it occurs,' he wrote, 'it is often managerially initiated'[33] in those authorities where the Labour Party supported compulsory unionism in principle and had at some time controlled the council for a long period. In keeping with his theory, however, the unions' lack of interest in the practice was attributed in part to their ability to organize without its aid, and in part to the generally placid nature of their relationship with the employer – both then typical of public-sector industrial relations. For instance, McCarthy reported a national officer of the Fire Brigades Union as stating that his union did not campaign for the closed shop 'because there was nothing in it for us'.[34] In addition, antipathy towards the closed shop existed among the highly unionized white-collar grades, particularly teachers who identified a clash between their professional status and compulsory union membership.[35]

Since McCarthy's study union interest in the closed shop has increased dramatically. Claims have generally been presented at local level, although in 1974 the manual unions discussed a national UMA and presented the idea to the employers. However, negotiations did not materialize because of a lack of uniformity in union organization and representation across the country and because the major unions concerned – NUPE, the T&GWU and the G&MWU – eventually opted to seek agreements area by area, suspecting that a failure at national level would hinder any subsequent local negotiations. Their hope was that once sufficient local UMAs had been secured, it would be possible to resurrect the issue of a national agreement. Even so, the effort at local level was hampered by overlapping recruitment territories. In authorities where union density was low and one of the unions predominated, it was sometimes reluctant to pursue a joint closed-shop agreement for fear of cementing the position of its weaker rivals and reducing the possibility of ousting them. Such considerations did not, however, apply to administrative, professional, technical and clerical grades where NALGO enjoyed a pre-eminent position.

To explain the closed shop's spread, we first examine the union side, looking in turn at the evidence to support our hard and soft theories. As regards the former, like workers in the nationalized industries, local authority employees found themselves in a more uncertain and hostile industrial-relations environment from the late 1960s onwards. The constraints of incomes policies, for example, provoked industrial action on a significant scale for the first time since the war. In 1969 and 1975 it involved refuse collectors in certain areas. In 1970 a nationwide campaign of selective strikes was conducted by the manual unions against the Conservative government's $n - 1$ incomes policy. During the 1978–9 'winter of discontent' the same unions mobilized support for a programme of selective action in pursuit of a pay claim that broke the Labour government's guidelines. Similarly, the Fire Brigades Union undertook industrial action in defiance of the 1973 incomes policy restrictions. Indeed, a nine-day unofficial strike took place in Glasgow. On a grander scale, a national strike by firemen stretched from November 1977 into 1978 before a formula could be found that satisfied the Fire Brigades Union without overtly breaching pay guidelines. This was probably the most dramatic event in the union's history. Although NALGO was not involved in such trials of strength, its growing militancy, as demonstrated by the 1970 conference debate over the introduction of a strike policy, took place against a background of unfavourable changes in salary levels relative to other white-collar groups, partly because local government officers were unable to exploit the productivity elements built into the incomes policies of the late 1960s. In the mid-1970s this discontent was compounded by threats to job security posed by local government reform. Strike action nevertheless was generally parochial. For example, NALGO's first official strike was in Leeds over the non-involvement of union members in a manual workers' bonus scheme.[36] Over all, a survey carried out in 1979 by Terry led him to conclude that strike incidence in local authorities, especially among manuals, was 'high in comparison to many sectors of private manufacturing industry' and that it was 'not fanciful . . . to describe local government as a new "strike-prone" sector'.[37]

Such a change would, according to our hard theory, generate closed-shop demands. Indeed our research into an Inner London Borough's NALGO branch revealed that interest in a UMA centred on an occupational group that had been involved in a strike and subsequently pushed the closed-shop issue at branch meetings, albeit unsuccessfully. Likewise, as early as 1961, the Fire Brigades Union conference passed a motion in favour of the closed shop. Subsequent conferences confirmed this policy. Yet until the membership's first taste of industrial action in 1973 hardened attitudes towards non-unionists, little was done to enforce it because the union's executive felt that closed-shop claims would be resisted by the majority of employers and that there was insufficient rank and file support to overcome it.

Such circumstantial evidence has to be treated with caution. To support the hard theory, the closed shop needs to be perceived by those involved as a practical means of increasing the effectiveness of strike action. Yet among firemen, a homogeneous and disciplined group, voluntary support for the union's stand was immense. Non-participators were little more than an irritant. In this instance, therefore, the increased interest in the closed shop might be seen as an expression of irritation at such 'free riders', of a feeling that they should not be allowed to get away with it. Although there is a fine line to be drawn between the two theories on this point, the firemen fit more comfortably into the soft theory in so far as there was little scope for the closed shop to raise already high levels of solidarity. A more plausible case for the hard theory can be made in relation to manual grades where solidarity across a diversified and scattered workforce of caretakers, cleaners, school meals and parks staff, home helps, refuse collectors, roadworkers and so on has been more elusive. But even here the vanguard in any industrial action has tended to be strategic groups like refuse collectors who traditionally provided the core of union solidarity, often to the extent of operating long-standing informal closed shops in London and the industrial conurbations. Nevertheless, while the full-time officials interviewed made little mention of the practice as a means of increasing strike effectiveness, it might be expected that union activists' interest in it was partly based on the hope that its presence would encourage reluctant members to support any future industrial action. Even if the threat of dismissal after loss of union card was an empty one because management would resist such a sanction and because it could not be imposed unilaterally, this does not mean that the seeds of doubt could not be planted in members' minds as to the consequence of ignoring a strike call.

Verification of such an argument is difficult. It is easier to build a case to support the second strand of our hard theory which associates the closed shop with the need to overcome serious union recruitment and retention difficulties. The manual workforce in local government, estimated to be 1.1 million in the mid-1970s, was not only occupationally diversified and geographically scattered, but also contained a high proportion of women (65 per cent) of whom 85 per cent were part-timers.[38] The latter included a quarter of a million school meals staff, a similar number of school cleaners and 100 000 home helps. For such employees contact with union officials and lay activists was often irregular, they were isolated from the main centres of union strength, and they were often apathetic towards union membership. Yet, while they were not crucial to any collective action, they worked under terms and conditions negotiated by the unions and were seen as a source of revenue. Indeed a great deal of effort went into recruiting them and with some success. In 1974, before closed shops became common, overall union density in local government was estimated to be 86 per cent, a surprisingly high figure. That partially explains why membership gains were not spectacular. For instance, of the written UMAs in our survey, 40 per cent were concluded when union density was at 90 per cent or above, while only one in ten came into effect when density was below 60 per cent. A second reason was that the great majority excluded existing non-members and therefore did not immediately increase coverage. Moreover, under some agreements significant numbers of part-timers – the very employees unions found difficult to recruit – were also exempt. A third reason was the perennial closed-shop irony that precisely in those areas where a union most needs the closed shop to boost membership, it is often too weak to force the issue, not least because management is usually more reluctant to comply when unionization is low. Thus the eight UMAs secured by the Fire Brigades Union were in urban authorities or in counties with industrial traditions where the union was strongest, while in the rural counties, where non-membership was more of a problem, claims had invariably been rejected.[39]

So, even though union officials interviewed identified increased membership as a significant incentive behind their efforts to secure closed-shop agreements, many of their successes were achieved in authorities where union organization was well developed. The implication is that much of the closed-shop activity in local government merely tidied up the membership position. UMAs were the product of high levels of unionization rather than a means of achieving it. Such evidence lead us towards our soft theory as a more appropriate explanation of closed-shop growth in this sector.

Further evidence for the soft theory is derived from an analysis of the changing nature of the unions involved. During the 1970s the three major manual unions adopted policies that placed increased emphasis on the role of the shop steward,[40] and led to the development of shop steward structures akin to, although less well developed than, those in the manufacturing industry. In his study of such organizations, Terry stresses that the effectiveness of the shop stewards in overcoming the problems of organizing and representing a fragmented workforce depended not on the existence of a closed shop, but on a peripatetic 'key steward' whose access to a car or a van allowed him to keep in touch with other stewards, and by means of pre-planned itineraries or fixed 'surgeries' was accessible to members with grievances. 'In the absence of such contact', Terry suggests, 'union membership often became a paper label; a condition of employment if there was a union membership agreement, or a gesture if there was not'.[41] Terry's study dispels simplistic notions of how stewards' influence and power works, and in so doing parallels Batstone *et al.*'s research on factory-based shop stewards.[42] Certainly the mere achievement of a closed shop was not the solution to the organizational problems related to a scattered work-force. That is not to say that stewards were uninterested in securing UMAs. One of the frustrations experienced by stewards in local government was that many important bargaining issues were dealt with nationally. The closed shop, on the other hand, was a local matter. Tabling a closed-shop demand helped fill a gap in the negotiating agenda and the achievement of a UMA could be regarded as a bargaining success. Moreover, as our soft theory stresses, the potency of the closed shop as a 'symbol' of stewards' new status should not be underestimated. Although concrete evidence for this view is difficult to secure it is pertinent to mention that in the industrial areas where closed-shop demands were most virulent, the local authorities absorbed labour from declining industries like coal-mining, shipbuilding and engineering and these workers brought with them trade-union traditions, including moral attachment to the closed-shop principle, which had hitherto been lacking among local government workers.[43] A similar argument can be made in relation to the Fire Brigades Union. Whereas the previous generation of firemen had often been recruited from ex-servicemen, the latest generation was much more likely to have been drawn from industries where trade-union activities and principles were commonplace.

To determine the balance of evidence between our hard and soft theories, employer attitudes are crucial. Employers' stances on the issue were frequently determined, not by industrial-relations considerations, but by the political complexion of the council. Labour-controlled councils were far more sympathetic to closed-shop requests than Conservative. The split was on a matter of principle. Labour councillors were more likely to share the kind of moral attachment to the practice shown by trade unionists. Conservative councillors tended to object to compulsory unionism on the grounds that it was an infringement of personal liberty. The closed-shop pattern generally followed these attitudes. Even so, the division was not hard and fast. Closed shops did exist under Conservative authorities, although these tended to be informal rather than written. And not all Labour councils endorsed the closed-shop principle. Some resisted claims for UMAs. Moreover, even though employer initiative in Labour areas was less significant than in McCarthy's day, there were instances of Labour councils being willing to concede a closed shop, and the offer being rejected by the unions concerned because of the objections of their members. This was particularly important in administrative, professional, technical and clerical grades. For example, in 1977 the Labour-controlled Greater London Council offered the GLC Staff Association a UMA. It balloted its members on the issue and the proposal was rejected. Similarly, in a London borough where we undertook some detailed research, a UMA had already been agreed in principle by the Labour council and the NALGO branch committee when a branch meeting voted on a show of hands against its introduction. Other instances of NALGO members voting to reject proposed UMAs occurred at Walsall and Stirling, while a ballot at Lothian Regional Council secured a majority of one in favour of a closed shop being introduced, a decision later reversed. There have also been examples of NALGO members challenging UMAs after they have come into operation. In 1979 members of Strathclyde Regional Council narrowly voted in favour of retaining a 'tight' closed-shop agreement.[44] At Sandwell District Council the dismissal of Joanna Harris under another 'tight' UMA in 1981 provoked a membership revolt in which the NALGO branch voted to withdraw unilaterally from the agreement, despite opposition from the other signatory unions and the employing authority. Indeed, the council refused to terminate the UMA.

The typicality of these incidents may be debated, but they do increase our fragmented knowledge of popular support for closed shops in the absence of widespread ballots. Equally illuminating is the fate of several UMAs where local councils have changed hands. When control has passed from Labour to the Conservatives UMAs have been withdrawn or diluted. In 1978, for instance, the Greater London Council came under Conservative control and approached the manual unions to renegotiate the existing closed shop, not because it was seen to make the unions too powerful in the bargaining sense, but to secure greater freedom of choice for employees. The council proposed that certain part-timers should be excluded, that other unions should be recognized by the authority to increase competition among the unions for the benefit of their members and that non-membership should be allowed on grounds of deeply held personal conviction against belonging to any union. The unions successfully blocked the first two demands and obtained a compromise on the third as the wider conscience clause was to apply solely to new employees. Less successful were the unions at Thameside in Manchester when in 1977 the incoming Conservative council withdrew a UMA introduced by the previous Labour council. Similar moves by Derbyshire and Nottinghamshire County Councils were thwarted when the unions persuaded management to accept revised UMAs containing wide conscience clauses. In none of these cases was there significant rank and file resistance to the changes.

The importance of the above examples is twofold. First, employers in local authorities have opposed the closed shop on grounds of principle rather than on grounds of its likely impact on industrial relations. Indeed, of the professional managers who responded to our survey and who were involved in day-to-day industrial relations, the largest category saw neither advantages nor disadvantages in practical terms. Second, and again with a caveat on typicality, they give some indication of the extent of membership support for the closed shops, which appeared limited.

Although there is some support in the local authorities for our hard theory in terms of increased union militancy and the scattered workforce problem, this latter evidence appears to tip the balance towards the soft theory. Employer concern has mainly focused on the moral issues involved rather than the closed shop's practical implications for industrial relations. Moreover, the moral stance of the employing council has determined where and when closed shops have appeared because rank and file agitation accompanying closed-shop demands has been limited. Rarely has it been strong enough to overcome employer hostility even though a new generation of activists has felt the symbolic importance of the practice, while in many authorities where the closed shop has appeared, it has done little more than tidy up an already high level of union membership.

PRIVATE-SECTOR MANUFACTURING

Once we move away from the public sector, the problem of identifying reasons for the spread of the closed shop becomes even more complicated because of the fragmented nature of private-sector collective bargaining. Although industry-wide negotiating machinery exists, closed shops have been concluded at that level only in a few cases. More typically, closed shops are negotiated domestically (see Chapter 2).

According to McCarthy, the bulk of the post-entry closed-shop population in manufacturing was concentrated in engineering and associated metal-working industries, printing and textiles where there were also substantial numbers in pre-entry shops.[45] Fifteen years later the practice had become far more broadly based, mainly as a result of the spread of post-entry arrangements. Areas of substantial growth included food, drink and tobacco, from 35 000 to a minimum of 266 000, the chemical and allied industries, from 35 000 to at least 156 000 and clothing and footwear from 40 000 to in excess of 83 000. Even so, these figures suggest that the closed shop is far from universal in this sector. Over all, the closed-shop coverage in manufacturing had reached only 40 per cent by the end of the 1970s, although this represented over half the total closed-shop population.

In explaining the spread of the closed shop away from its traditional enclaves, one factor of paramount importance has been succinctly described by William Brown and his colleagues' at the Industrial Relations Research Unit (IRRU) in their study of changing bargaining contours in manufacturing:

Ten years before our survey, industrial relations in manufacturing industry was dominated by multi-employer agreements . . . By 1978 that had been transformed. For two-thirds of manual and three-quarters of non-manual employees the formal structure of bargaining has become one of single-employer agreements covering one or more factories within a company . . . By the late 1960s the problems that came from informal, fragmented bargaining were painfully obvious to most managements. Whether or not they were aware that they were doing so, they set about following the reforming prescriptions of the Donovan Commission. Our survey shows that there was a great increase in the professionalism of management's approach. There are now many more specialist industrial-relations managers in positions of responsibility than there were a decade ago, and their interests are far better represented on boards of directors . . . The consequences of single-employer bargaining for trade unions have been far reaching. The shop steward has moved from the wings to the centre of the negotiating stages. Particularly in larger establishments . . . stewards now have complex organisations and strong procedural recognition . . . To some extent the stewards' achievements have come from their own efforts, helped by a more sympathetic attitude on the part of their union leaderships. But the support given to workplace organisations by management has been enormous. Closed shop arrangements have spread far from their traditional industries and now cover almost a third of the manufacturing workforce [our figure is higher]; three quarters of these arrangements are openly supported by management. The deduction of union dues by management, comparatively rare ten years earlier, was in operation for almost three-quarters of union members in manufacturing by 1978. The number of full-time shop stewards probably quadrupled over the decade, so that they now far outnumber the full-time officials on trade unions' own pay-rolls. The proliferation of full-time shop stewardships appear to be particularly dependent upon managerial policy, tending to mirror the degree of specialisation of the industrial relations function.[46]

This analysis does not in itself predispose us to either the 'strong' or the 'weak' theory of closed-shop growth. Which is more appropriate depends on the role the closed shop played in this reform. Looking for support of the hard theory, we might begin by contrasting the sophistication of shop steward organization found by the IRRU survey with the informal, unofficial and often unconstitutional nature of steward activity during the 1960s. Despite some acceptance of their lubricating role, stewards commonly met employer hostility during that period. Often too they encountered the disapproval of union officialdom. While striving to bring consistency to the erratic, opportunistic aspirations of the rank and file, they were hampered by organization that was seldom more than rudimentary and sometimes by the precariousness of their personal positions. In such circumstances, a closed shop forced on reluctant management would have helped demonstrate stewards' authority. Undoubtedly this happened, especially in those industries like engineering with a shop steward tradition, the practice acting in the classic McCarthy manner to further trade-union solidarity and organization.

However, the IRRU survey carries a rather different message. Using its data, Hart emphasizes the closed shop's importance in maintaining not solely shop stewards' organization, but also the system of joint workplace regulations to which management lent support.[47] Such an analysis remains within the hard theory, the 'substantial' benefits derived from the closed shop being shared by both managers and shop stewards. It was to their mutual benefit to secure union boundaries, increase union membership and promote union control over the rank and file.

Securing union boundaries and avoiding or ameliorating problems associated with multi-unionism would seem to have been of particular benefit in the fragmented pattern of unionization in manufacturing, especially during the period of competitive union recruitment in the late 1960s and 1970s. Use of the closed shop in this way was most graphically seen in the negotiation of 'green site' agreements. Where a new factory was being built, an employer might select a union and negotiate with its officials a comprehensive procedural agreement, including a closed shop, prior to hiring the workforce, so that all recruits had to join the specified union as a condition of employment from the outset. The intention behind this move was threefold. First, in areas where union traditions were strong and therefore unionization was considered inevitable, management had the opportunity to pick a union that was considered by other local employers to be 'responsible'. Second, the in-plant pattern of unionization was not left to chance and the disruptive effect of competing unions trying to prove themselves to potential members was eliminated. Third, the fact that one union had a high degree of security and its disciplinary procedures covered all employees was thought conducive to strong leadership by stewards and full-time officials and hence to stable industrial relations.

A second significant example of employers' finding advantages in securing boundaries and increasing union membership through the closed shop occurred in a number of declining industries such as clothing, footwear and textiles, and to a lesser extent tobacco. Dwindling employment in these sectors jeopardized the financial stability and the continued independence of a number of quasi-industrial unions, for example, the National Union of Tailors and Garment Workers (NUTGW), the National Union of Footwear, Leather and Allied Trades (NUFLAT), the Amalgamated Textile Workers Union and the Tobacco Workers Union. As membership threatened to shrink in proportion to the diminishing size of the workforce, these unions showed a keen interest in securing the closed shop as a means of achieving a compensatory increase in union density. Several of these unions suffered from the problems of organizing a scattered, high turnover workforce (over 45 per cent per annum in clothing manufacture) and were too weak to force closed shops upon the employers. Employers began to recognize the problems and became sympathetic to the unions concerned. The Clothing Manufacturers' Federation, for instance, developed UMA guidelines in 1976 to encourage individual companies to recognize the closed shops as a means of protecting the NUTGW, even though the union itself was tentative in claiming such agreements. Its justification was that the union understood the problems of the industry, had participated in joint delegations to the government and the EEC, and had co-operated in measures to improve the competitiveness of the industry. The hope was that closed-shop agreements would not only boost NUTGW membership, but also limit the penetration of such general unions as the T&GWU into clothing, and avoid the necessity of the NUTGW having to merge with a larger union because of lack of revenue.

The reasons behind the closed shop in footwear were similar to those in clothing, although NUFLAT had showed itself a rather more robust union than the NUTGW. It enjoyed very high-density levels until the job contractions in the industry were compounded by the erosion of membership as individuals exercised their right not to belong to a union under the Industrial Relations Act. In fact between 1970 and 1974 membership dropped by 10 per cent. Once the Act was repealed the union took up their long-standing closed-shop campaign with renewed zeal, threatening a strike in 1975. Despite the reluctance of a number of firms, the employers, through the British Footwear Manufacturers Federation, conceded an industry-wide UMA in 1976, partly on the grounds that NUFLAT's continued viability and independence was important to the generally peaceful industrial relations in the industry.[48]

Such examples reflect a general acknowledgement of the mutual benefits derived from the conclusion of a closed-shop agreement to protect unions already *in situ*. Related to this means of defending a recognized union's territory against incursion by 'foreign' unions is the policing of that territory. A major reason why management in manufacturing lent support to the development of shop steward organization was to provide them with the wherewithal to ensure rank and file compliance with agreements and to deter unconstitutional action. Hart,[49] as we have noted, sees the closed shop as an instrument in this process. She emphasizes its ability to create a settled union province from which dissident groups cannot escape. Nor can they use such a threat to force stewards to meet their demands. Take the example of a factory in which management and shop stewards have concluded a productivity deal which seeks to implement major changes in working practices, the effects of which fall unevenly on the various departments within the factory. Employees in one department may choose to resist the introduction of the agreement because it has a particularly harmful effect upon the custom and practice built up within their workshop. But without any alternative official access to management or the opportunity to secure alternative sources of union representation, or even to resign in protest from the union and then perhaps to encourage other dissatisfied members elsewhere in the factory to do the same, their opposition is likely to remain a local protest. Confident, moreover, that no membership will be lost, stewards may take a harder line with such renegade groups than they would in an open shop. If the rest of the factory has been persuaded to accept the productivity deal and is working to its provisions, the steward leadership is in a strong position to cultivate rank and file antagonism towards the dissenters to the point where they become isolated and eventually ready to return to the fold. Should they turn to unofficial action, the stewards, as a last resort, might even feel secure enough to permit management to draft union members from other departments to cover their jobs. This kind of argument mirrors that which emerged in the railway industry in the late 1960s.

How far does our own evidence support this hard theory view of closed-shop growth in manufacturing? Of the enterprises whose management representatives were interviewed in our research, seventy-two were primarily concerned with manufacturing. Most were large multi-plant companies and together they covered a wide range of manufacturing activities. From the in-depth interviews carried out we were able to determine the attitude they adopted when faced with a closed-shop demand somewhere within the company. Such attitudes varied considerably. For example, thirteen of these companies were found to display a strong dislike for the closed shop and opposed demands wherever they arose. A few of these were also hostile to trade unionism generally, but others were heavily unionized. Some even tolerated the existence of closed shops where they had taken over a company with such practices but were not prepared to enter into new UMAs. A further four companies were also against the closed shop in principle but had come to accept it as unavoidable in some areas. They did not have so rigid a stance when faced with new demands. In addition, two companies were determined to resist the further spread of the closed shop within their organizations. So, altogether one in five of our sample were unsympathetic to closed-shop demands. Of the remainder, fourteen were doubtful about the appropriateness of compulsory unionism for white-collar workers or for certain categories of them. This left about half the sample with no objections to the closed shop in principle for any category of employee, treating each claim on its merits or laying down criteria that the union needed to meet in order to secure a UMA. For instance, twenty-nine firms stipulated minimum union density necessary for management to contemplate a closed shop, although in some circumstances they were willing to be flexible.

What can be gleaned from these findings? First, even at the high point of closed-shop growth in the late 1970s there remained substantial opposition in manufacturing firms to the practice. Particularly pertinent were the four companies that accepted closed shops on pragmatic grounds, but displayed hostility to them in principle. The ambivalence was due to a divergence of opinion between the specialist industrial-relations managers and the board of directors and/or line management. This may have been the tip of an iceberg, hiding the extent of managerial disagreement over the closed shop. However, the expediency of the industrial-relations function held sway in the late 1970s and all four firms had concluded extensive UMAs with their unions.

Second, even where management took a more favourable attitude towards the practice, this was not an unconsidered 'we think the closed shop is marvellous' approach. Apart from the Co-operative Wholesale Society, no firm had taken the initiative in thrusting the closed shop upon unions, except occasionally on 'green sites'. Even those companies that laid down density guidelines appropriate to considering a closed shop were cautious in determining the percentage figure, a caution that has important implications for our hard theory.

As limiting the number of unions within a plant and protecting existing unions was regarded as an important contribution by the closed shop to 'stable and robust joint regulation', our management question-naire included a specific question to find out whether managers viewed compulsory union membership as a means of limiting the number of unions in the plant or company. In the manufacturing firms with experience of closed shops, 44 per cent affirmed that the practice was indeed useful in preventing encroachment by outside unions. Yet there was often a discrepancy between this reply and the reluctance of those who ventured it to consider a closed-shop agreement at anything but high levels of union membership. Many were unwilling to be more specific than to regard a substantial union density as a prerequisite for a closed shop. But twenty-nine stipulated in their policy guidelines a rough percentage of the workforce which the union/s ought to have recruited before management would seriously discuss union member-ship as a condition of employment. All considered it inappropriate to negotiate a closed-shop agreement until union density exceeded 70 per cent in a defined bargaining unit, and thirteen refused to contemplate a closed shop until union membership had passed the 90 per cent mark. This indicates reticence in using the closed shop tactically to avoid multi-unionism. A company that regarded the closed shop as performing such a function might be expected to consider it at lower densities when the preferred union was less well established and when an outside union stood a greater chance of recruiting a solid membership bloc. If no infiltration had occurred by the time the resident union had recruited 80 to 90 per cent of employees, then the likelihood of subsequent incursion would be remote, especially if the established union's position was shored up by Bridlington, by sole bargaining rights, by clearly delineated spheres of influences, by check-off, by access to new entrants and other aids to union recruitment and security which are part and parcel of a comprehensive factory agreement. At that stage a company was either saddled with multi-union representation or had avoided it and the introduction of a closed shop was largely irrelevant to the pattern of union organization.

Equally pertinent is the fact that 46 per cent of the private-sector sample had not seen and had not used the closed shop as a method of combating multi-unionism. Sometimes this was because the company had not experienced or feared inter-union rivalry. In other cases, multi-unionism was already a fact of life when closed-shop agreements came to be concluded. Interestingly there was no great difference between the density guidelines mentioned by this group of managers and the group that answered positively to the union encroachment question.

A telling factor in this argument is management's attitude to white-collar UMAs. The reluctance to conclude non-manual UMAs extended to many firms that took manual UMAs in their stride. Indeed, white-collar UMAs remain extremely rare in private-sector manufacturing, despite the growth of white-collar unionism. Yet this has been an area of intense union competition, involving not only specialist unions like ASTMS and APEX but also the white-collar sections of manual unions. It might have been thought that judicious concession of loose UMAs would have offered management a much more orderly pattern of union representation and a chance to avoid the multi-union jungle characteristic of many blue-collar workforces. However, management appears to have baulked at this strategy.

It might be inferred from these cautions density guidelines that when the workforce was unorganized to the extent that the union/s concerned would make dramatic recruitment gains from the closed shop, management tended to be unwilling to conclude a UMA despite its theoretical strategic value at this early stage of workplace unionization. Such reluctance may have been based on the idea that union growth should develop stage by stage. Passing from one stage to the next may properly be accelerated by a favourable stance towards the union, but stages ought not to be leapfrogged by the premature introduction of a closed shop, nor ought management to do the union's recruiting job for it. It may also have been reinforced by a mistrust of the closed shop principle by boards of directors and managers outside the industrial-relations function, which tied the hands of industrial-relations managers. It may even have been that industrial-relations managers' suppressed mistrust of the practice prompted them not to concede a UMA prematurely, especially as closed-shop demands at relatively early stages of unionization could be resisted with comparative ease.

Such an analysis leads us away from the hard theory towards the soft theory. The closed shop begins to appear as one of the final pieces in the jigsaw of joint regulation, having been conceded only when the bulk of the workforce was recruited and the stewards securely bound into joint institutions, whereupon it may have been introduced to mop up the last pockets of non-unionism. Often, in fact, it did not even do this. With few exceptions, the managers interviewed stressed that they sought to exclude existing non-unionists from compulsory membership when negotiating UMAs and our research into the content of such agreements confirmed the extent to which this objective had been achieved.[50] Indeed it could be argued that trade-union acceptance of such 'liberal' UMAs has reduced management opposition and thus facilitated the spread of the closed shop in private-sector manufacturing.

The preceding analysis has important implications when the disciplinary function of the closed shop is considered. High-density guidelines would also suggest that employers were less than convinced that their caution should be set aside to make way for the disciplinary advantages of compulsory unionism. This view was reinforced by our interview programme. On the one hand, very few managers felt that in conceding closed shops they were increasing stewards' control of their members to the firm's cost. On the other hand, although a quarter of respondents with experience of closed shops judged that stewards' authority was increased in the company's interest, most admitted that from their experience of existing closed shops, the benefit was 'theoretical'. Indeed, few were willing to concede that an expectation of any changes in their industrial-relations climate for good or ill had figured in their response to union demands for the practice. Most of the companies contacted owned a large number of plants and must have had long experience of informal closed shops at least at one or two locations. As industrial-relations reform was introduced within the company and formal UMAs were contemplated as part of that movement, at first expectations of advantages may have been high, as was found to be the case in certain nationalized industries in the 1968−71 period. But, as management became more familiar with the contribution of UMAs to the new system of joint regulation, expectations became tailored to reality. New demands for closed shops were judged on such criteria as union density, the category of workers involved, particularly whether or not they were white collar, and how 'liberal' an agreement could be obtained. Industrial-relations factors, such as union security and orderly relations and union power, became less prominent in managerial calculations. Indeed, provided a number of safeguards and caveats were adhered to, managers appeared to become increasingly blasé about closed-shop demands. Such demands were expected and dealt with in many cases by applying a stock response tried and tested in other plants. They came to expect no significant advantages or disadvantages from the appearance of a UMA. Any advantages were an unexpected bonus, while experience taught them that formal UMAs with wide exemption clauses and detailed appeals procedures minimized confrontation with individuals. Isolated problems may have been accepted as a risk, but they were expected to be a rarity rather than a constant nagging worry. Elaborate procedures often remained unused and minor difficulties were sorted out informally without recourse to dismissal, as management discovered that the vast majority of employees and potential employees preferred not to jeopardize their jobs in defence of a perceived freedom not to belong to a union.

Did the trade unions become so blasé? This is difficult to assess. The problem in ascertaining the extent and nature of trade unionists' feelings about and expectations of, the closed shop was related to the form that recent arrangements took and the method by which they were established. Rank and file participation in the demand for, the establishment of, and the operation of a closed shop was greater in the kind of practices that McCarthy observed than in the UMAs of the late 1970s. The degree of management resistance encountered in McCarthy's closed shops meant that practices often only won recognition after a period of unilateral enforcement – by union members refusing to work with 'nonners', by sending them to Coventry or by other sanctions – until the individuals either took out union membership, left, or were sacked. On the very first page of his book, McCarthy quotes such an instance. 'The shop did stop; and I think we stood there for about four hours. I remembered this man was particularly brave. He stood there for all of those hours and watched us losing pay. It was a shocking 240 minutes but all the time he just stood there.'[51] In some cases attempts to secure a closed shop by such methods went on for years so that by the time the employer was prepared to acknowledge the arrangement, rank and file resolve had been tried and tested. In coal-mining, printing and dockworking, for instance, the hostility generated during this process endures today even though workers may not have encountered a non-unionist in their workplace for decades.

By contrast, the establishment and functioning of the modern UMAs did not necessarily require a great deal of effort by the rank and file trade unionists. The request for a closed shop was often formulated within the shop steward hierarchy without prior agitation on the shop-floor. Once introduced, its operation became the responsibility of detached administrative arrangement, involving check-off, the sifting of job applicants by the personnel department, and ultimately the routine dismissal of those determined not to join or to leave the union. In many cases the rank and file rejection of non-members proved to notional, enshrined in perpetuity by jointly agreed procedures after only the most tentative of demands for the practice. Its existence remained unproved. Union members had no opportunity to demonstrate to management that they would not work with non-unionists because management was playing an active role in ensuring that they did not have to do so. On the rare occasion where a 'nonner' slipped through the net or a protest resignation occurred, the procedure moved into action and the problem was resolved without the rank and file having to raise a finger to defend the closed shop.

Yet from the late 1960s onwards closed-shop demands came thick and fast in manufacturing, which suggests, if not popular support, then at least acquiescence in the introduction of the practice, perhaps based on the feeling that 'free riders' ought to join the union and pay their subscriptions. For shop stewards and other activists who provided the main impetus behind the closed-shop movement there is little doubt that the fact of having a closed shop was important. This was not so much a matter of mopping up non-unionists. Shop stewards were frequently willing to forgo this advantage in order to win managerial acceptance of the practice. Nor was it merely a matter of union security. As the IRRU survey discovered, management support in terms of check-off, sole bargaining rights, time off for union duties, payment of full-time conveners and so on ensured that stewards enjoyed a high degree of security and influence within the plant. Nor was it a matter of increasing their control over the workforce. As Batstone *et al*'s study of a large motor factory revealed, shop-steward power over the workforce was an immensely complicated process of formal and informal rules and networks.[52] In the smaller factories found in the food, paper, brewing and rubber industries, all of which have seen the closed shop become commonplace in recent years, shop-steward influence is even more intimate. Conveners are less remote than in giant plants, and many would know a significant proportion of the workforce personally. One convener interviewed, for example, argued that the work groups that were likely to be most critical of him, and most likely to challenge agreements and break procedure, were also the most union conscious within the factory, the core of union solidarity. If there had been no closed shop, they still would have been unlikely to resign from the union because they disagreed with the steward's decision. They would protest from within and set about voting the convener out of office. Moreover, the convener admitted that even if they were to resign, he could not use the closed-shop sanction against them. It was not his business to preside over mass sackings of people he knew well and whom he regarded as good trade unionists.

In such contexts, the closed shop's appeal to shop stewards was less tangible than the functional advantages it might have offered. In engineering plants, for example, shop stewards pursued the closed shop almost because it was expected of them in an industry where such practices were traditional. It was a ritual they needed to go through to prove their status as trade unionists. In multi-plant companies where the closed shop was spreading, the same argument applied, as shop stewards in 'open' plants became conscious that stewards elsewhere were securing UMAs. In industries that lacked a closed-shop tradition, the ritual may have been an even more significant endorsement of the new bargaining responsibilities and autonomy of the shop stewards, as formal plant bargaining began to replace industry-wide negotiation. Especially in the food and brewing industries where the T & GWU factory branch system freed stewards from the impositions of geographically based union organization, the closed shop was an expression of their independence. It meant that they could say to new employees 'if you come into this factory, you join this factory branch'. The focus of identity was on the factory, not the wider trade union, and hence upon the shop-steward body and not the union full-time officials and the union hierarchy. The closed shop, in contrast to its traditional craft and industry-wide scope in printing, coal-mining, shipbuilding and the docks, came to symbolize for many shop stewards the parochialism of factory-conscious trade unionism in which they were the key figures.

SUMMARY

In explaining the growth of the closed shop in the nationalized industries, local authorities and private-sector manufacturing in recent years, we sought to determine which of our hard and soft theories was the more convincing explanation of the growth of the practice over the past twenty years.

The 'strong theory' emphasizes the functional importance of the closed shop in industrial relations either as a trade-union weapon to overcome organizational problems or to promote strike solidarity, or as a joint union/management weapon to promote stability, order and discipline. The 'weak theory', on the other hand, challenges the functional importance of the closed shop, seeing it rather as a marginal factor in industrial relations, a side-effect of procedural reform, perhaps playing a tidying role where union membership is already high, and an expression of trade-union traditions and values rather than a practical weapon in trade-union action.

We found evidence to support both theories. But two key features stand out from the complex picture. The first is that the process of closed-shop growth must be viewed historically. In the 1960s when managerial hostility to closed-shop demands was prevalent, there was more evidence for the 'hard theory' in so far as trade unionists and employers were prone to identify the closed shop as the union weapon of tradition. This was especially true of the nationalized industries and manufacturing. Closed shops were slow to emerge at this time because, despite union agitation, management resistance was strong. Towards the end of the 1960s, however, management attitudes began to change. A need for industrial-relations reform and productivity bargaining brought an influx of industrial-relations specialists and a recognition that the closed shop could be of mutual benefit to management and unions in their search for stability and order. The nationalized industry UMAs of the late 1960s and early 1970s were crucial in furthering this idea and started a spate of closed-shop activity that was cut off by the Industrial Relations Act in 1971. Its repeal in 1974 led to a resumption of this activity at an accelerating pace. But as the closed shop became more commonplace, our soft theory became more relevant. Able to judge the performance of closed shops already in existence, management became less certain of its advantages, yet continued to concede UMAs where union membership was high because they could see few disadvantages and accepted that it fitted in with the logic of formal joint regulation. In addition, because unions were willing to accept 'liberal' UMAs, management could expect few problems with individuals. From the union side, the success of closed-shop campaigns elsewhere encouraged activists to seek their own arrangements, because of residual organizational advantages, because of resentment against 'free riders', and because of its symbolic importance. The more the closed shop spread, the more routine became closed-shop negotiations. The more routine closed-shop negotiations became, the more the closed shop spread. Familiarity bred further UMAs.

The second key point is that the soft theory can be seen as a diluted version of the hard theory. Between these two extremes there are degrees of adulteration, depending on particular contexts, but the factor common to them all became 'maturity' in industrial relations; the stress on procedural consensus, on mutual interests, and on institutionalized conflict. The exact role of the closed shop within this setting may vary or be difficult to identify. Yet the crucial factor is that it has not been seen as a weapon that can be used to breach the norms of the system. Where different norms prevail, it was seen as just such a weapon with resultant management hostility. For example, in manufacturing, a number of firms were eager to minimize the role of trade unions within their organizations, and with this went a deep distrust of the closed shop. But where the norms of 'mature' industrial relations existed the closed shop increasingly became, to use a phrase of one of our respondents, 'part of the furniture', unless there was some special, frequently moral, reason why the employer disliked it.

6 The Operation of the Post-entry Closed Shop: Impact on Management and Industrial Relations

INTRODUCTION

The previous chapter indicated that a key factor in the recent spread of the closed shop was a reduction in managerial hostility towards the practice. How far has management experience of its operation justified this reappraisal? Here we examine the available evidence.

MANAGEMENT PERCEPTIONS OF THE IMPACT OF THE CLOSED SHOP

The most decisive evidence relating to the closed shop's value to management was provided by the Warwick survey of manufacturing industry which found that three-quarters of employers with experience of closed shops saw advantages in the practice, while only a half saw disadvantages.[1] Less clear were the results of our own survey of Engineering Employers' Federation (EEF)-affiliated establishments.[2] Whereas on perceptions of disadvantages there was some similarity between the two surveys on the advantage side, the engineering survey found only 53 per cent of managers with experience of closed shops considered they derived benefits from them. There were, however, a number of differences between the two studies. First, the engineering industry is a traditional closed-shop industry where many informal, long-standing practices existed and where management was less inclined to think of the practice in terms of benefits because the closed shop was considered a 'fact of life'. Second, the Warwick survey encompassed many sectors where the closed shop was a new phenomenon and where managers had been involved in weighing up the closed-

91

shop issue while negotiating UMAs. Hence there may have been a greater tendency to see such arrangements in positive terms. Third, the two studies were carried out in different ways. Whereas the engineering survey was postal, Warwick's was undertaken by market research interviewers which may have encouraged managers to be more forthcoming.

Table 6.1 shows the contrasts and similarities of the two surveys but also reveals the problem of non-replies in our postal survey. A number of respondents who reported having closed shops left the questions relating to advantages and disadvantages blank. If these are discounted the proportion of those who saw advantages rises to 63 per cent, closer to the Warwick figure, while the number recognizing disadvantages rises to 58 per cent. However, it would be unwise to assume that this absence of replies meant that the managers concerned were unable to think of advantages or disadvantages. That may have been the case, but, equally, it could have been that they were not prepared to devote any time to answering the questions.

The Warwick survey separated its responses relating to manual and non-manual closed shops. The EEF survey made no such distinction. It found relatively few non-manual agreements and all those managers who had concluded non-manual UMAs also had experience of manual arrangements. The EEF responses to open-ended questions were categorized as far as possible to compare with those used by Warwick's. The problems of such categories as 'helps stabilize relationships' is that they are vague enough to cover a multitude of possibilities. The Warwick survey encountered the same difficulties and its three most significant advantages were catch-all categories, just as was the EEF major advantage.

The significant feature of the EEF survey was the variety of advantages and disadvantages expressed. Apart from the broad first category, the single most widely expressed advantage was that the closed shop removed 'free rider' disputes. This, in effect, is the least a closed shop might be expected to do by its very nature, the least management might expect to gain from a closed shop. On the other hand, one of the major potential advantages, the enhancement of trade-union authority over dissident work groups or unofficial strikers, received little support (5 per cent). However, in both surveys it is difficult to know whether this benefit was implied by those managers who said that the closed shop was important in ensuring stability or in ensuring that all workers were covered by one procedure. Hart suggested that this is a significant factor, quoting the defence of the closed shop by the Central Electricity

TABLE 6.1 *The Warwick and EEF surveys: advantages and disadvantages of the closed shop as seen by managers*

Warwick survey	Manual %	Non-manual %	EEF survey	% n = 167
			Advantages as seen by managers	
Ensures that the union represents all workers	41	27	Ensures one negotiating body, and one channel of communication	26
Helps stabilize relationships	21	45	Protects established unions	4
Procedures cover all workers	14	10	Increases union authority to management's advantage	5
			Helps relations between established unions	4
			Removes 'free rider' disputes	19
Union card provides evidence of apprenticeship	3	—		
Others	10	15	Others	5
No advantages	28	20	No advantages	36
			No reply	11
More than one response	16	17	More than one response	13
			Disadvantages as seen by managers	
Increases union strength	14	23	Increases union strength	13
			Worsens relations between unions	4
Creates inflexibility in dealing with individuals	13	7	Creates inflexibility in dealing with individuals	10
Infringes individual liberty	9	7		
Restricts recruitment	11	13	Restricts recruitment	16
Others	10	5	Others	7
No disadvantages	49	50	No disadvantages	42
			No reply	14

Generating Board in the Ferrybridge case.[3] A similar uncertainty clouds the responses relevant to the most widely accepted management benefit. Both Weekes[4] and the IPM[5] emphasized the value of the closed shop to management in protecting the established union/s against poaching and in limiting multi-unionism. Yet only 4 per cent of the EEF sample explicitly mentioned this advantage. This was probably because a multi-union pattern was already established in the engineering industry and in many cases closed-shop agreements arrived too late to affect it. While the Warwick survey did not offer the avoidance of multi-unionism as a separate category of benefit, Hart made it clear that the 'helps stabilize relationships' advantage referred *inter alia* to the protection of favoured unions from outsiders and the avoidance of multi-unionism. She reported, for example, that the majority of recent closed shops in the Warwick sample applied to a single union.[6]

On the disadvantage side, the most widely cited cost of the closed shop to management in the EEF survey was the restriction on recruitment (16 per cent). This response, however, was affected by the fact that the survey covered both pre- and post-entry arrangements and in engineering the former, which would tend to put a greater limitation upon selection choice, was particularly common. The same proviso applies to the Warwick survey. Otherwise, the two surveys indicate that the most frequent problem that management found was that the closed shop increased union strength to the firm's cost. Under this general heading the EEF survey included growth in the influence of militants and the fostering of restrictive practices. It is nevertheless perhaps significant, in the light of public comment on the closed shop, that such a small proportion (13–14 per cent) of industrial relations managers should have felt that the closed shop brings an unwelcome enhancement of union strength.

The value of the two surveys lies in giving a general picture of management attitudes towards the closed shop. In particular, despite the variety of advantages and disadvantages offered, the frequency with which managers saw no advantages and/or no disadvantages in the practice suggested that the closed shop has had less impact on industrial relations than has often been suggested. According to the EEF survey, 18 per cent of managers judged the practice to offer neither advantages nor disadvantages, while about a quarter balanced the two. Of the remainder, the bias was in favour of the closed shop. About a quarter saw only advantages whereas 17 per cent saw only disadvantages.[7] Yet both surveys were limited in the quality of information they produced. It is difficult, for example, to distinguish between major and minor benefits and costs, and to evaluate the practice within the system of industrial relations in the establishments involved. For that reason, we attach particular importance to our programme of interviews with managers, the results of which are reported below.

Of the 115 managers interviewed in the private and public sectors, 94 had experience of the closed shop on which they were able to comment. They represented a broad range of the largest employers in the UK. The sample was drawn from the 100 largest private companies in Britain, according to 'The Times 1000', supplemented by a variety of smaller firms thought to be typical of a trade or industry, and the nationalized industries. The interviewees were usually industrial-relations specialists.

The responses to open-ended questions about managment's attitudes were divided along the lines already described in the EEF survey. A quarter (26 per cent) appeared indifferent towards the pracice, seeing neither major advantages nor major disadvantages in the closed shop in which they were involved. Taking a balanced view, 21 per cent weighed advantages against disadvantages. Over a third (35 per cent) looked upon the closed shop favourably in so far as they noted benefits but not any signficant costs, whilst 17 per cent were hostile, reporting disadvantages that were not offset by significant advantages. These findings acord with the EEF survey, although rather fewer managers appeared indifferent to the practice, and there was a significantly greater proportion whose stance on the closed shop was benign.[8]

Perceived Advantages

Table 6.2 breaks down the reported advantages into categories comparable to the Warwick and EEF surveys.

The higher proportions responding to each category reflect the fact

TABLE 6.2　*Advantages of the closed shop as seen by managers: interview programme*

	%
Increases union authority to management's advantage	21
Protects established unions	46
Helps relations between established unions	30
Procedures cover all workers	19
Tidies up industrial relations	17
Removes 'free rider' disputes	20
Others	18

that during an interview management inevitably dealt with the subject in more depth than when asked to complete a postal survey. In all, 40 per cent of managers saw no major advantages, although about a half of these acknowledged some minor advantages.

Increases Union Authority to Management's Advantage

Although a fifth of managers claimed this to be a benefit, they offered little evidence to substantiate the view. A third of those who mentioned this gain admitted that it was theoretical, while others qualified their judgements with such comments as the closed shop made the union more confident or it gave the union some psychological hold over the membership or it improved relations between union and management. Two respondents went as far as to say that the practice diluted the influence of militants. But, even though one manager argued that without the closed shop there would be anarchy, no one could quote an instance where the firm had colluded with its union(s) to bring about the expulsion of groups of members who had refused to conform to agreements or procedures. The expulsion/dismissal combination had been mobilized on rare occasions against as individual, but to use it against groups of dissident workers seemed to be regarded as wholly inappropriate.

The consistency of this evidence suggests that the use of closed-shop agreements by management and union representatives to expel and dismiss disorderly groups of employees plays little part in management industrial-relations tactics. In any case such a tactic would be fraught with dangers. For the union there might be a blacklash from other members antagonized by an action that appeared to be a conspiracy between management and the union leadership, and aware that the same weapon could be turned on them in the future. Equally, management might realize that it would be difficult to secure the co-operation of the union in such a venture, which was likely to involve some soul-searching among its representatives. It would, for example, present shop stewards with a difficult decision, for condoning the dismissal of their own members may have ramifications for their relationship with the remainder of the rank and file, and in the long run for the robustness of the management/steward relationships.

There is more evidence to suggest that management considers the closed shop to have some disciplinary value in inhibiting members from 'voting with their feet' when they feel the need to express dissatisfaction by resigning from the union either to join another union or to become non-unionists. In so doing the closed shop is seen as giving union officials the confidence to make unpopular agreements relating to productivity and to eliminate restrictive practices and other major changes in working arrangements, and the confidence to see these changes implemented. However, evidence from our survey is less than conclusive. On the one hand it was found that, especially in the late 1960s, a number of companies introduced extensive and complex productivity deals requiring a high degree of co-operation by union officials and shop stewards in which the closed shop was conceded as a component of the package.[9] It was a managerial hope that compulsory union membership would 'put more muscle behind the agreement'. On the other hand, the evidence also suggested that during the 1970s the association between the search for productivity and the conclusion of closed-shop agreements broke down. A higher proportion of closed shops were introduced in isolation or as part of a pay package without productivity strings. Moreover, management optimism about the impact of the practice in facilitating change tended to dwindle during the 1970s. This suggests that, even though a closed shop might have some initial effect in making union representatives more co-operative, as the practice becomes 'part of the furniture', its significance diminishes. A small number of managers did comment that they were realizing that the closed shop did not provide a safeguard against resistance to change. Where the closed shop becomes a given feature of the union/management relationship it would appear to begin to lose its impact. Its novelty and coercive potential is reduced.

The interview programme showed that where long-standing closed shops existed, management often found it difficult to assess its disciplinary effects. One, for example, said that it was 'difficult to imagine life without the closed shop'. Even where closed shops had recently been introduced managers were wary of claiming significant disciplinary gains. Although they might have had pre-agreement hopes, some felt that it was too early to tell. Others argued that there were too many other factors involved in union discipline or indiscipline to isolate the closed-shop variable. Overwhelmingly the impression obtained from the managers interviewed was that the closed shop could not change weak union leadership into strong leadership. In one factory, the industrial-relations manager admitted that the union representatives had always had a limited influence over the rank and file both before and after the introduction of a UMA. In another organization, it was felt that the unions had always regarded membership discipline as an important priority and although a clause was written into the UMA stressing that union officials would do everything in their power to curb membership disorderliness, such an undertaking had already been accepted by the unions and the closed shop did little to reinforce this stance.

Where instances were found of groups of workers taking unofficial action, the closed shop had no influence. The members involved had no wish to leave the union as part of their protest and the union was unable to bring them into line. The desire not to leave was a crucial point. For the closed shop to prevent union members 'voting with their feet', those members have to want to 'vote with their feet' or at least to consider it as an option worthy of consideration. How frequently is this the case? In the late 1960s there were examples of groups of members defecting from recognized unions to join or set up breakaway unions, for example, in British Rail, the Post Office, Pilkington Glass and the Central Electricity Generating Board. All of these companies eventually introduced closed-shop agreements. But, more generally, while in open shops apathy may create problems of lapsing, the instances of militant groups of workers resigning or threatening to resign from their unions as part of their tactics of increasing or protecting their job control, or in demonstrating their dissent from official union decisions, do not appear to be at all widespread. Dissenting activities have been carried out firmly within the context of union membership. In Britain industrial relations have been characterized by the degree of autonomy enjoyed by shop-floor trade unionists and the limited control that union officials have been able to exercise over them. Yet there is little or no record of such groups of members needing to express this independence by resigning from the union. Within the framework of trade unionism there is ample room for work groups to pursue their own goals, ignore established grievance procedures, and express disagreement with their union officials without the need to abandon the loyalty towards the union. Indeed in those industries where informal work group activity has developed most, for example in the docks, in motor manufacture, in shipbuilding, coal-mining and printing union consciousness and the valuation of union membership has also been observed to be highly developed. According to McCarthy they were also the sectors where the functional value of the closed shop was most prized. Dissent and independent unofficial action seemed perfectly compatible with a strong attachment to union membership. The recent spread of the practice into areas of weaker trade-union traditions has not altered this relationship. If a workplace has a record of what management considers unruly behaviour by groups of workers, the introduction of a closed shop will not usually alter such behaviour merely because those involved can no longer 'vote with their feet'.

Given the dominant traits of British industrial relations it was hardly surprising that only 21 per cent of managers interviewed expressed any faith in the disciplining powers of the closed shop and that many were able to express this faith only in the most general terms. Comments included:

'Stewards are freer in their problem-solving activities.'
'The union can be more realistic in its approach to problems.'
'The union is more sure of its ground.'
'There are gains in goodwill.'
'The closed shop creates a greater *sense* of order.'

In short, managers generally found the discipline advantage to be intangible. They felt it was there, or sensed it without being able to quote concrete instances. When asked directly whether they thought the closed shop reduced the number of unofficial strikes or the number of breaches of procedure, none were prepared to say yes, while only a handful were willing to say that they had noticed any change in union bargaining attitudes since the introduction of a closed shop.

Procedures Cover All Workers

In struggling to express their feelings on the practice's impact, managers tended to stray into lesser advantages. For example, 19 per cent felt it was beneficial that the same set of procedures covered all employees in a particular grade, without indicating that the procedures were more readily observed because of this, or that those who had previously been outside the union had been prone to taking independent collective action parallel to that of unionized workers. This latter behaviour appeared to be rare. Those who remained outside the union when density reached 70, 80 or 90 per cent tended to be identified as either apathetic towards membership, unwilling to be collectivized or reluctant to pay union dues especially when they were receiving the same pay rises as those who did contribute. Collective agreements on terms and conditions negotiated by unions are almost invariably intended to cover members and non-members alike in a particular bargaining unit. Although in open shops unionists have sometimes pressed for member-only benefits, management agreement has almost never been secured. There is no evidence to suggest that non-unionists in heavily unionized grades have banded together to negotiate their own distinct agreements. The benefit of the closed shop in this instance therefore seemed to relate to management being able to treat all employees alike, through the medium of their union representatives, eventhough many UMAs allow non-members to stay outside the union and outside union/management procedures.

Tidies up Industrial Relations and Removes 'Free Rider' Disputes

Some 17 per cent of managers felt that UMA tidied up industrial relations. It regularized the position on union membership, taking it out of the realm of uncertainty and informality and incorporating it into the sphere of formal joint regulation by defining precisely the obligations and rights of employees and by defining who was obliged to join or stay in the union as a condition of employment and who could remain non-unionists. To an extent this formalization also helped reduce the tensions between members and non-members even where non-members continued to exist. Of the managers interviewed, 20 per cent acknowledged that the introduction of the closed shop had removed niggling 'free rider' wrangles, although as far as recent UMAs were concerned, few had been preceded by strike action to force management to dismiss those who would not join the union.

Protects Established Unions

Although the distinction between the membership and discipline functions of the closed shop is analytically useful, there is overlap between them. For example, when union members 'vote with their feet' because union membership is not a condition of employment, they become ripe for the attentions of other unions seeking a toehold in the enterprise. Given that inter-union rivalry and a chaotic pattern of union representation has been a feature of British industrial relations, it is scarcely surprising that almost half of the managers interviewed (46 per cent) felt that one of the beneficial effects of the closed shop was to protect recognized unions from the poaching of 'foreign' unions. The fear of unwanted unions entering the company was a less decisive reason for management conceding the closed shop than has sometimes been argued, because management was often reluctant to introduce closed shops at a low union density (see Chapter 5) and because agreements on sole bargaining rights, access to new employees, check-off, and spheres of influence, coupled with the Bridlington Principles, often went a long way towards making the membership function of the closed shop redundant. However, once the closed shop was conceded, it was clear from the interview programme that the practice's continuation became valued by management because its removal would have reopened the possibility of inter-union competition occurring or recurring. In other words the closed shop came to be valued as a desirable *status quo,* its presence preventing an uncertainty that management wished to avoid.

Helps Relationships between Established Unions

Closed shops widely exist in multi-union bargaining units. where more than one union is a signatory to the UMA. In these circumstances how far does the signing of such an agreement benefit management by reducing the unions' need to compete over membership and recruitment? How far does the signing of a UMA help define spheres of influence whether between co-signatories or between signatories and non-signatories where such boundaries are ill defined? About a third (30 per cent) of managers interviewed noted some favourable effect in this direction, although on the question of better definition of spheres of influence between co-signatories, the closed shop tended to act as a catalyst in resolving difficulties rather than solving them in itself. The negotiation of the closed-shop agreement was used by a number of firms as an opportunity to force the unions to consider ways in which spheres of influence might be clarified, the objective being to produce a separate agreement on the subject as a precondition of management accepting compulsory unionism. Yet in many cases, where the membership of unions was too intermixed to formalize spheres of influence adequately, informal arrangements for sorting out who should recruit whom usually continued after the introduction of the closed shop. Members sometimes continued to swop unions and new employees were allocated a union depending sometimes on where they worked or sometimes merely on which union appealed to them. In fact it appeared that the closed shop had little effect in either improving or worsening this type of situation, unless management had succeeded in concluding a separate sphere of influence settlement. As regards the relations between signatory and non-signatory unions and blurred boundaries between them, a few managers felt that the closed shop had helped stabilize those boundaries especially as legal considerations demanded a clear definition of the class of employee covered by a UMA.

Perceived Disadvantages

Table 6.3 Breaks down the reported disadvantages into categories generally comparable to the Warwick and EEF surveys.

TABLE 6.3   *Disadvantages of the closed shop as seen by managers: interview programme*

	%
Increases union strength	15
Worsens relations between unions	16
Creates inflexibility in dealing with individuals	25
Restricts recruitment	15
Encourages restrictive practices	15
Others	12

The table includes major and minor disadvantages. Many respondents provided more than one disadvantage. In all, 62 per cent of managers interviewed saw no major disadvantages although a third of these noted some disadvantages.

Increases Union Strength

About one in seven managers felt that the closed shop increased union strength to the enterprise's cost or had a potential to do so. Half of these were generally happy with existing closed-shop arrangements but felt that compulsory union membership nevertheless made the company vulnerable to militants taking control of the union, although this had not happened in practice. One manager suggested that such a takeover was less likely to happen where a closed shop operated, but that if it did the effects would be worse than in an open shop because people would be more easily led in directions in which they did not want to go. In another organization, the Co-op, long distinguished by its pro-closed-shop stance, it was felt that a cost of this ideological commitment to 100 per cent unionization was the enhancement of union bargaining power, especially in the retail trade where its competitors were not generally heavily unionized. Another firm felt that since the concession of a closed shop in 1967, its union had grown stronger, although it was difficult to isolate the closed shop's significance in this process. The most hostile company had had long experience of formal closed shops. During the 1970s its industrial relations had become increasingly volatile, culminating in a national strike in which the union had sought to expel strike breakers in the hope that management would eventually sack them in accordance with their UMA. Unwilling to face this prospect, management rescinded the agreement. Of the remainder, two were construction firms that operated informal closed shops on various sites but did not encourage the practice, judging that in the industrial relations perculiar to building sites, where the unions often have to re-establish their organization at each new location, the closed shop was likely to increase their bargaining power by overcoming organizational difficulties and stabilizing membership. Even so, one admitted that where closed shops did exist union officials were sometimes willing to adopt a more conciliatory attitude than they would when they were still struggling to recruit members. Finally, two companies, whose hostility towards the closed shop showed itself in a refusal both to formalize existing informal practices and to concede new UMAs, included among their reservations about such arrangements the argument that they strengthened the union to an unwelcome degree.

The conclusion from these findings is that managers with experience of the closed shop did not generally consider it to enhance union strength to the firm's cost. When asked directly whether the closed shop had contributed to a greater frequency in strike activity or in lengthening strikes that did occur, only one firm agreed that this was the case. Part of this unwillingness to make any firm judgement on the impact of the practice in this area could be attributed to managers being unable to compare open shops with closed shops because the latter had existed for a long time or being unable to evaluate the effects of a UMA that had recently been introduced. Nevertheless, the evidence that this was not perceived by management to help shift bargaining power towards trade unions remains persuasive. It is especially pertinent that among those few managers who went against the prevailing opinion, a significant portion belonged to companies that were not prepared to co-operate actively in the operation of the closed shop, merely allowing it to exist informally where unions had established 100 per cent membership. Perhaps this indicates that where the closed shop is imposed unilaterally by union members and where it is associated with conflict rather than collusion, it can in certain circumstances have a more damaging effect on management's interests than in a context where it is subject to the compromise of a jointly controlled UMA. In this latter situation, the closed shop appeared as an everyday background part of the union/management relationship and was associated with continuity, stability and union security rather than with trade-union coercion in an industrial dispute. Partly this has been due to the nature of modern UMAs which have often been introduced without conclusive proof of mass-membership support. Managers often expressed confidence that the union would be unlikely to mobilize sufficient support to force the company to dismiss strike breakers and those that the union intended to expel, and therefore felt they could veto the use of the UMA in such a way. In addition, managers often felt that union representatives would be unwilling to test closed shops to possible destruction[10] for fear of jeopardizing their long-term role in stabilizing union membership by eliminating the constant effort needed to recruit and retain members. Even so, in an industrial dispute the closed shop's impact is not confined to providing an *ex post facto* punishment for strike breakers. Its existence can deter people from disobeying a strike call. The threat need not be articulated by union representatives. There need only be an awareness on the part of members that failure to respond to union instructions would risk future reprisals. However, managers generally seemed unconcerned about this possibility, either because the deterrent was not regarded as effective in so far as employees continued to defy the union in such circumstances, or because, when a strike became inevitable, some merit was seen in having the entire workforce withdrawing its labour. This latter point of view was supported by such managerial arguments as the residue of employees who refused to join the strike merely caused a bitterness that poisoned the atmosphere long after the strike was over, and this residue did not necessarily perform a useful function during a strike and often had to be sent home anyway. Indeed some managers regarded it as a virtue that everybody should support a strike once it became inevitable.

In theory the closed shop might be expected not only to increase union discipline to management's cost during a strike. A few managers indicated the danger of the practice enabling militant union officials to force an apathetic rank and file to condone union stances they would not willingly support. It might be argued that if union and management reach deadlock in negotiations and offer a proposed agreement for the judgement of the union members, then union officials who want the proposals rejected can use the closed shop as a means of cajoling employees to vote against them, especially if the vote is taken by a show of hands rather than by secret ballot. However, managers generally seemed unconcerned by this possibility. To some extent they felt confident that they would be able to deflect the threat by refusing to contemplate sacking anybody expelled from the union under such circumstances, a confidence strengthened by the knowledge that such a threat would only become crucial when the union was in a position of weakness, unable to command willing majority support. Equally, experience taught managers that union representatives did not seek to affect their members' behaviour in this crude way, preferring less drastic methods of persuasion through the formal and informal networks by which stewards and other officials disseminate their views and try to shape members' opinions. Some managers even went as far as to say that, where non-militants have been drawn into the union by a closed-shop agreement, union officials may have to be more sensitive towards moderate opinion because it becomes more numerically important. This was not a widespread view however. The prevalent opinion was that it was impossible to make hard and fast assumptions about the relative militancy or moderation of union representatives and the rank and file. It would be misleading to presume that union leaders, at any level, are more aggressive and unconstructive in their attitude towards management and use the closed shop to herd union members along militant paths. Over all, managers did not emphasize the disciplinary potential of the closed shop against the firm's interest.

Worsens Relationships Between Unions

Almost a third of managers interviewed felt closed shops improved relations between unions that were established in the organization. On the other hand, 15 per cent thought that it worsened such relations. The main problems in this area related to workers moving from one grade into another. For example, one problem mentioned concerned the promotion of craftsmen from skilled manual grades covered by pre-entry shops into supervisory grades for which specialised white-collar unions, like the ASTMS, had concluded post-entry UMAs. Rather than join the white-collar union, the promoted craft workers often wanted to retain their craft union cards because they were important in ensuring future job mobility in trades where pre-entry practices were common. Such dilemmas occasionally caused friction between the two types of union involved. Although one solution was often the holding of dual membership by supervisors, this was not always possible because some craft unions frowned upon the arrangement or their rules specifically forbad it. Other inter-union difficulties mentioned by managers included attempts by a general union that had signed UMAs covering semi-skilled and unskilled workers to use the agreements subsequently as a means to try and oust craft unions from maintenance and other skilled grades in the same plant. This was particularly acute where the general union concerned already had some membership among skilled workers and was able to exploit uncertain spheres of influence. It felt able to claim that the UMA concerned gave it sole rights to recruit, represent and negotiate for all manual workers including craftsmen.

The resultant bitterness between the unions involved had, from management's viewpoint, unwelcome repercussions on their industrial relations. Indeed, in order to avoid such inter-union squabbles, firms have often insisted upon spheres of influence being settled in tandem with the UMA. The remaining problem mentioned, albeit minor, was the cementing of inter-union rivalries by the introduction of a closed shop. A small number of managers felt that where relations between unions were already bad, the effect of the closed shop was to hamper the reconciliation of the rivals by formalizing the barriers between them. This was expressed nebulously, however, and on the whole disadvantages relating to inter-union relations tended to be niggling rather than of major significance.

A number of these inter-union problems were brought to the attention of the TUC by affiliated unions. In the late 1970s its Disputes Committee examined several cases where unions felt that their 'organizational rights' had been prejudiced by other affiliates entering into formal union membership agreements with management. Between 1977 and 1979, six such cases were dealt with and, although the Disputes Committee was able to find satisfactory solutions, the TUC expressed concern about affiliated unions making closed-shop agreements without considering the interests of other unions in possible breach of the 'TUC Disputes Principles and Procedures'. It led the TUC to include in its *Guide on Trade Union Organization and the Closed Shop* the advice that when making closed-shop agreements or arrangements unions should have regard to the interests of other unions who may be affected and should consider their position in the drafting of the agreement.[11]

Some TUC unions also expressed disquiet that other affiliates were accepting requests from managements to organize new establishments from 'front door to the back door': that is, they were being offered a closed-shop arrangement even though national agreements or other arrangements in other establishments of the company already provided for multi-union recognition. This, together with the problem described above, led the National Graphical Association to propose a motion to the 1978 TUC Congress urging a review of the effectiveness and utility of the TUC Disputes Procedures that should include consideration of avoiding disputes between affiliated unions arising from UMAS, particularly where a number of affiliated unions were involved in the appropriate negotiating machinery.[12] The motion was carried and the General Council subsequently recommended that there should be a note of guidance in the TUC *Disputes Principles and Procedures* that affiliated unions, when making UMAs or sole negotiating rights arrangements, should have regard to the interests of other unions that may be affected. Where unions could not resolve these matters themselves the General Council recommended they be referred to the TUC for advice and conciliation, and if necessary to the Disputes Committee for adjudication. In 1979 Congress accepted this recommendation which was then incorporated into the TUC Disputes Machinery as a note to Principle 1.[13]

The overwhelming majority of managers did not consider the post-entry closed shop to be a hindrance to labour flexibility when it required crossing from one union territory to another. On the question of internal labour flexibility generally, the same view applied. Where problems did exist the bulk of managers did not associate them with the closed shop.

Encourages Restrictive Practices

Only 12 per cent of managers interviewed thought the closed shop encouraged restrictive practices. In this category the most frequent problem mentioned was that recognized unions insisted that sub-contracted labour, usually hired to undertake specialist work on site, should be fully unionized. Difficulties were said to arise when either the subcontracting firm or its employees refused to comply with this condition. Nevertheless most managers did not regard these problems as insuperable. Some insisted that the whole difficulty could be avoided by writing the condition of union membership into the original contract before any subcontracted labour arrived on site. Others said that even this was unnecessary as subcontractors normally kept a drawer full of selected union cards that they doled out to employees working in sensitive areas. Otherwise the evidence that the closed shop encouraged restrictive practices was flimsy. Two respondents felt that the closed shop was consistent with a restrictive environment, although not a cause of it, but most managers who acknowledged that restrictive practices did exist in their organizations felt it too complex a problem to be pinned at the closed shop's door.

However, the Conservative government elected in 1979 was concerned about the growth of the practice of union labour-only requirements in commercial contracts. It argued that such requirements were a means of spreading the closed shop to companies and employees who did not want the closed shop and perhaps to employees who did not want to be represented by a union at all. The practice was also viewed as restricting competition because it prevented companies from tendering for and obtaining work for reasons that had nothing to do with whether they could do the job competently and competitively. The government's opinion was that the decision on whether a company secured a contract should be decided on its merits and not on whether the company had a closed shop or employed union members. The Employment Act 1982 stipulated that discrimination against non-union firms in the awarding or making of contracts was unlawful and removed legal immunity from those who organised industrial action against non-union firms and their employees. Following the publication of the proposed Act as a Bill, a number of local authorities were revealed to be insisting that contractors had to recognize and negotiate with trade unions if they were to gain contracts. The government felt that the effect of such requirements was the same as union labour-only contracts. They forced union recognition on companies who did not want it and excluded non-union firms from tender lists and contracts. Consequently it introduced new provisions into the Bill to make requirements on recognition and negotiation unlawful and to provide redress for those who suffered from such restrictions.

Creates Inflexibility in Dealing with Individuals

The most widely expressed disadvantage related to management's concern for the individual and to problems of dealing with individuals in closed shops. One in four managers considered that the closed shop created or could create inflexibilities in dealing with individuals. This response was related to management style or the personal feelings of managers interviewed. The companies of those managers who raised this issue were not more prone to difficulties associated with individuals than others. Three-quarters of them had not been forced to dismiss employees in the past ten years because of the operation of closed-shop arrangements. Moreover, among managers who held this reservation were some of the strongest supporters of the practice because of its utility in collective terms, the caveat being appended to their generally favourable stance. Indeed one manager emphasized the value of compulsory union membership in allowing the company to deal with employees on a collective rather than an individual basis, but then bemoaned the fact that management could no longer listen to the voice of the individual. More commonly, managers offered moral objections to the practice as an infringement of individual liberty, rather than practical objections in terms of having to dismiss individuals. Some thought the idea of having to sack non-members to be distasteful or embarrassing, while two said that their firm would refuse to dismiss anybody for non-membership and their closed shops continued because such a situation had never arisen.

In fact, while airing their theoretical and moral concerns about the closed shop, the minority who noted this disadvantage had very similar experience to those who did not. There was no evidence to suggest that their closed shops were tighter, their trade unions more intolerant and the problems arising either more frequent or more intractable than those of the majority of companies that felt that they had protected individual interests to their own satisfaction. Firms in both groups had commonly developed UMAs in conjunction with their unions to limit the possibility of individual problems through a variety of safeguards including exemption for existing non-members and appeal procedures. More significant perhaps was the infrequency with which such procedures have been used. The large majority of managers had not encountered major problems with individuals, particularly problems that placed the company in a position of having to dismiss employees. No managers interviewed had encountered constant recurring problems.

DISCUSSION

The broad conclusion from the preceding analysis is that the impact of the post-entry closed shop on industrial relations tends to be elusive. The majority of managers interviewed were either unable to identify the costs and benefits involved with any certainty or considered them peripheral. They saw the practice as fitting in with an industrial-relations policy intended to cope with high levels of unionization through formal joint regulation over a range of workplace issues. In executing such policies, they tended to value the practice as a passive element in the *status quo*. Even if it was too cumbersome a piece of machinery to be employed actively in the complex relationship between the company, its union/s and its employees, it created a background of stable union membership that could be taken for granted. Its removal might have brought unwelcome uncertainty by renewing union membership as an issue, by increasing the possibility of inter-union competition, and by jeopardizing management's carefully constructed relationship with union representatives. As one manager summed up: 'The closed shop is rather like the monarchy. It's not what it does but what others might do if it wasn't there.'

Although this evidence is consistent with our explanation of the growth of the closed shop, it can be criticized on the ground that the managers interviewed were mainly industrial-relations specialists who may have had a vested interest in showing the UMAs they had conceded in the best possible light, or who may have been less aware of the day-to-day effects of compulsory unionism – especially where disadvantages were concerned – than were production managers. In reply, three points may be made.

First, if industrial-relations specialists were trying to 'whitewash' the closed shop, it might be expected that they would have been more favourable in their responses. To repeat a point made in the first chapter, assessing the impact of the closed shop does not involve comparing strong trade unionism with weak. The comparison is between voluntary and compulsory trade unionism, a more tricky exercise. Industrial-relations managers seemed aware of this fact. Their reluctance to attribute major costs and indeed benefits to the closed shop stemmed from an unwillingness to isolate such arrangements from the paraphernalia of practices and procedures that accompany 'mature' joint regulation in industry and a range of historical, economic, technological and social factors which determine the character of their relationship with the workforce.

Second, how far are the effects of the closed shop hidden from industrial-relations specialists because they only manifest themselves on the shop-floor where they become a line management problem? Have such specialists underestimated the contribution that compulsory unionism makes to restrictive practices? To answer these questions it is necessary to examine the nature of restrictive practices in relation to the way in which the closed shop might shape workers' behaviour.

Wherever trade unions are well organized, practices emerge that may be defined in management terms as restrictive because they curtail managerial prerogative. Such practices may result from concession in formal bargaining and be incorporated in the collective agreement. They might include manning levels that from the company's perspective are too generous and work-study values that are too slack. Industrial-relations specialists were likely to have been aware of these and taken them into consideration when estimating the impact of the closed shop. In so doing they appeared to see them as a consequence of strong trade unionism rather than of compulsory membership. Equally important, however, are the restrictive practices that arise informally on the shop-floor out of attempts by workers to affect the effort required of them in the work process, to improve terms and conditions, and to protect jobs. Because such rules tend to exist in unwritten custom and practice, it could be argued that industrial-relations specialists are likely to be less familiar with them than line managers whose control over the workforce is affected by them constantly. How far might these be encouraged by the closed shop?

In pre-entry areas, especially where craft workers are concerned, it is true to say that the closed shop has been closely associated with such restrictive practices as craft demarcations, the refusal to allow semi-skilled workers to be trained to skilled level, the insistence that skilled workers only be employed on deskilled jobs because they are identified as 'belonging' to the craft union concerned and the blacking of work from non-union sources. But here we are concerned with the post-entry shop, the functions of which are more limited. Therefore our analysis must be different. Much has been written about custom and practice, especially in relation to the operation of bonus schemes and the restriction of output.[14] Its value and legitimacy among workers has been identified as strong. They maintain and extend it through social pressures on fellow workers which establish acceptable norms of behaviour, and unofficial sanctions against supervisors and line management. Indeed the closed shop was traditionally imposed in this way. However, in recent years the closed shop has entered the formal world regulated by written rules and written procedures. The modern UMA is divorced from custom and practice in a way that McCarthy's closed shops were not, which makes it an extremely cumbersome weapon in protecting and expanding custom and practice rules.

To demonstrate this, let us look how a written UMA may influence workers' actions. The basic mechanism is that those who fail to join, or who resign, lapse or are expelled from the union are dismissed by management after a formal procedure is exhausted. Its coercive effect depends either on this process being carried out, or on the knowledge that it will be carried out acting as a deterrent upon those contemplating non-membership or behaving in a way that would jeopardize their membership. Let us assume that a small number of workers are refusing to conform with custom and practice or have refused to participate in unofficial industrial action intended to protect it. If fellow workers threaten to have them expelled from the union, is it a realistic threat? Can it be carried out? To secure expulsions, the workers concerned would have to bring the issue to the attention of the formal world. They have no power to expel members themselves. That can only be done through the union's expulsion machinery which involves the union officials who are responsible for the written collective agreements with which custom and practice conflicts, and the formal procedures that the unconstitutional action, which they did not ratify, has broken. Moreover, even if by some chance the expulsions took place, the UMA would probably stipulate that management has the right to discuss the merits of an expulsion case with the unions and that the worker concerned has the right of appeal before being dismissed. Inevitably the union officials involved would find it difficult to justify the dismissal of people who had refused to act in breach of the substance and procedures of the agreements which they themselves had negotiated, or to sanction industrial action against the company if management refused to sack. Their credibility as negotiations in good faith would be destroyed. Finally, once the problem had reached this stage, industrial-relations specialists would have been all too aware of it. Of course it is impossible to be absolutely certain about the kind of threats that do alter workers' behaviour on the shop-floor. But there are much more immediate sanctions available to force conformity to group norms than the expulsion threat. They were documented as long ago as the Hawthorne studies[15] and involve a variety of expressions of disapproval from sarcasm to ostracism. In short, our suggestion is that restrictive custom and practice rules are the product of strong shop-floor organization not compulsory union membership. Their extent and durability depend on a variety of factors that cement group norms and permit work groups to pressurize line management including worker ideology and orientation to work, payment systems, strategic position in the production process, economic environment, management policies and control systems and the influence of union representatives over their members.[16]

Third, it must be remembered that the evidence upon which this chapter is based was collected in the late 1970s when many of the closed shops upon which managers were commenting were fairly new. It could be argued that their appraisal was based on a brief experience during which no opportunity had arisen to demonstrate its effect either to management's benefit or cost. One of the characteristics of the practice may be that it lies dormant between relatively infrequent occurrences where it can play a decisive role in industrial relations. To use the phrase of a manager interviewed: 'It's kept in the cupboard'. For example, in plant baking an industry-wide closed shop had operated in various forms since 1965 with employer co-operation. In 1978 a national strike call was defied by significant numbers of union members whom the union threatened to expel. The Bakers' Federation then withdrew the closed shop agreement and once the strike was settled refused to reactivate it.

Further evidence of such managerial reappraisal of the closed shop upon encountering a situation in which it seemed likely to act against employer interests appeared in 1982 in British Rail, British Airways and British Telecom. These are discussed more fully in Chapter 8. However, it must be pointed out that in all these cases managements' stance against being forced to expel members was successful – which suggests that either the closed shops relied heavily on management compliance and were not sufficiently robust to be controlled unilaterally by the unions, or their discipline function cannot work against large numbers of dissenters. Both possibilities would tend to confirm our interview findings that managers felt in control of their UMAs.

7 The Operation of the Closed Shop: The Union and the Individual Worker

Public concern has been expressed about how the individual worker is treated under closed-shop arrangements. Much of this disquiet has arisen from particular individual cases.[1] Concern has concentrated on four major areas. First, some have expressed the view that the closed shop is often introduced, and continues to operate, without the support of those working under such arrangements. Second, many argue that the closed shop results in individuals joining a union against their better wishes – a view expressed in 1981 by Norman Tebbit, Secretary of State for Employment:

Unless you can persuade people that the union is good for them, you ought to do something to alter the union. If you are only left with conscription and bullying to get people into the union there is something wrong with the union itself. I abhor all these conscription measures and bullying that go on through such things as the closed shop.[2]

Recognising such criticisms, the TUC has stressed that unions should place emphasis in membership recruitment on persuading workers of the benefits of trade-union membership rather than coercion.[3] Third, there has been concern that the operation of the closed shop results in individuals, some of whom may be long-service employees, losing their jobs. Such a loss arises in three situations. Individuals may be dismissed because they refuse to join a union when a closed shop is introduced into an open area. They may lose their job or be unable to take up a preferred job because they fail to gain admission to the appropriate union. They may also have their employment terminated in a closed shop through expulsion from the union for an offence against union rules or policy.

Fourth, some have suggested the compulsory unionism results in workers participtating in industrial action with which they disagree because they fear that to strike break will result in loss of union card and thus their employment. Mrs Thatcher expressed this view when she addressed the 1979 Conservative Party Conference:

> We are particularly concerned about the working of the closed shop. The closed shop, together with secondary picketing, makes it possible for small groups to close down whole industries with which they have no direct connection. Cross the picket line to do your job and you risk losing both your union card and your job . . . During the engineering strike [autumn 1979] news reached London of a new resistance movement in East Anglia. Whole factories were actually working, but so afraid were the employees of the consequences that they chose not to reveal their identity, or that of the company, to the media. Millions of British workers go in fear of union power. The demand for this Government to make changes is coming from the very people who experience this fear.[4]

How Far Have Closed Shops Been Introduced and Continue to Operate without the Overwhelming Support of Those Working Within Them?

While it might be said with some certainty that most of the traditional closed shops in printing, shipbuilding, coal-mining and various skilled trades were established through and still retain substantial levels of membership support, such support is more difficult to confirm where new post-entry practices have emerged during the past twenty years. Most were the product of the official collective-bargaining machinery rather than of unilateral shop-floor enforcement and operate through formal procedures that do not require membership involvement. The best measures of the popularity of such agreements among those covered would be the level of strike activity that had been necessary to secure them and the results of ballots to ratify them. Unfortunately the evidence available on these matters is only partially useful.

First, because of the reduction in management hostility towards the practice in recent years, the vast majority of new closed shops resulted from peaceful negotiations. Strikes to pressurize employers into conceding UMAs were rare. Indeed data provided by the Department of Employment (see Table 7.1) showed that over the period 1962–80 inclusive there were only eighty-five reported stoppages of work in

TABLE 7.1 *Strikes over the introduction of the closed shop, 1962–81*

Year	Number of stoppages	Number of workers involved	Number of working days lost
1962	5	1 606	3 480
1963	1	21	500
1964	2	600	2 400
1965	3	675	3 560
1966	9	11 439	25 608
1967	8	1 514	4 506
1968	7	1 015	5 693
1969	10	3 257	10 352
1970	14	3 714	16 726
1971	0	0	0
1972	1	11	17
1973	0	0	0
1974	0	0	0
1975	6	546	6 056
1976	5	330	3 436
1977	10	1 625	72 197
1978	1	20	400
1979	2	626	3 111
1980	1	42	525
1981	0	0	0
Total	85	27 041	158 567

support of the introduction of a closed shop. These involved 27 000 workers at a cost of 158 500 working days. The Department was unable to provide information on their outcome but, assuming that they were all successful, then their contribution to the net increase in the closed-shop population over this period was just over 1 per cent. Our EEF survey revealed a rather greater degree of conflict surrounding closed-shop demands. Seventeen per cent of practices were conceded only after industrial action was threatened or took place, reflecting perhaps the strong closed-shop traditions in the industry encountering equally traditional employer wariness, especially over pre-entry shops which tended to be particularly contentious. Even so, this relatively low incidence of disputes offered little insight into the general level of support for compulsory unionism.

Second, as regards ballots the evidence is patchy. Although work-force votes to sanction closed-shop agreements were not unknown in the period under consideration, sometimes, especially in the early phase, the issue was presented to employees as part of a package deal so that it was difficult to isolate it from, say, the pay and productivity proposals that accompanied it. More broadly, referenda varied considerably in form. While secret ballots appeared to have been a rarity, union officials did not negotiate UMAs in a vacuum. The groundswell of opinion was often made plain to them through resolutions to conference (see Chapter 5: section on nationalized industries) and through branch votes. Admittedly, low participation rates in branch activities may have meant that the mandates of conference delegates and the substance of branch decisions did not accurately reflect rank and file opinion. Yet it cannot be assumed that the result was inevitably in favour of the closed shop. In the water industry, for example, NALGO dropped its claim for a white-collar UMA when soundings amongs the branches revealed its unpopularity among the membership. Similarly, in the London Borough of Southwark the issue generated sufficient feeling to ensure a well-attended NALGO branch meeting at which, on a show of hands, members decisively rejected a branch committee recommendation to conclude a UMA with the already willing employer. Post Office engineering offers another example. Consistently the POEU's Conference has rejected calls for the union to adopt a closed-shop policy, debates becoming increasingly lively during the late 1970s as union members tasted industrial action. Such examples are indicative of the fact that, even in the absence of ballots, union activists could not ride roughshod over rank and file opinion. This was especially true in white-collar areas where the limited penetration of the closed shop was partly due to activists being unable to mobilize membership support and partly due to a managerial sensitivity towards employee feelings. For instance, when the General Council of British Shipping was approached by the Merchant Navy and Airline Officers' Association for a post-entry shop it sought to measure officers' views by writing to them individually. In this case only sixty-four expressed opposition. The GCBS thus concluded an agreement with the MNAOA which exempted from compulsory union membership those who had dissented.

Although still the exception rather than the rule, ballots were more common in white-collar than in manual grades. Sometimes the results were surprising, even to management. For example, when faced with a union demand for a closed shop, an insurance company confirmed in writing that it would concede such an agreement if employees voted in favour by a simple majority on a minimum 66 per cent turn out. It assumed that this target was beyond the union's reach. However, of the

72 per cent who voted, 1402 supported the proposed UMA and 602 were against it. More generally, results of ballots have reflected the controversial nature of the issue among white-collar employees, especially in the local authorities (see Chapter 5). In Walsall and Stirling, for example, NALGO members voted against UMAs. Members of the GLCSA also rejected a closed shop proposal in 1976. The majority was two to one against among white-collar grades, although schoolkeepers voted three to one in favour. Elsewhere ballots resulted in closed shops being accepted, usually by narrow margins. Lothian Regional Council saw a majority of one, while the NALGO ballot at Sandwell Metropolitan District registered 810 for a UMA and 671 against. The volatility of workers' attitudes towards compulsory membership was, however, a significant factor, as demonstrated by the following occurrence in the paper industry. During 1979 the white-collar union at a paper mill raised the closed-shop issue with management. Management were willing to comply provided 70 per cent of those to be covered were in favour. Despite the fact that union density was high, the vote fell narrowly short of the required target and the matter was dropped. Later in the year a strike, unrelated to the closed shop but lasting several weeks, took place. In 1980 the closed shop was raised again and another referendum was conducted. This time well over 90 per cent favoured a UMA. Changes in attitude, although in the other direction, also occurred in local authorities. Lothian NALGO members later reversed their initial majority of one in support to a majority of fifty-eight against. At Sandwell, in the wake of Joanna Harris's dismissal for non-membership in 1981, the NALGO branch voted by a sustantial majority to withdraw from the UMA it had concluded in the previous year.[5] At Strathclyde Regional Council, although no poll had previously taken place, rank and file pressure forced the union to hold a ballot on the continuance of an existing UMA. The result was 5214 in favour of the arrangement and 5024 against in a 68 per cent turn out. The result was, however, disputed. Controversy surrounded the fact that the qualifying date that governed whether NALGO members could vote (31 October 1978) was some eight months before the ballot, allegedly disenfranchising between 1500 and 2000 unionists who had joined after 31 October mainly as a result of the UMA. Opponents of the UMA argued that these 'conscripted' members would have been likely to tip the balance against the closed shop. NALGO's defence of the October qualification was that it coincided with the qualifying date for voting in the election for the union's national executive council.

The above are isolated examples. Even though many UMAs

contained clauses relating to periodic, sometimes annual, reviews, none
that we came across expressly stated that a ballot should form part of
this review. This was despite advice from some employers' associations
that management should seek such provisions during negotiations.[6]

The rarity of strikes and ballots over the closed shop prevent us from
drawing any firm conclusions on the degree of popular support enjoyed
by the practice. What other evidence exists? The most obvious sources of
information are opinion polls of which there have been many in recent
years. To an extent these were discussed in Chapter 4. In general, trade
unionists' attitudes vary depending upon the precise question asked,
although the bias is towards disliking compulsory membership from which
it might be inferred that closed shops do not have the mass support of
those under their jurisdiction.[7] The counter-arguments to this are that
trade unionists may respond differently to general questions about
compulsory unionism than they would when asked to decide upon the
specific closed shop that they are involved in; that their attitudes to their
closed shop may fluctuate depending upon the circumstances surrounding it, as the Sandwell and paper industry examples demonstrate; and
that in being asked to acquiesce in it, they are not necessarily having to
condone full-blooded 100 per cent compulsory trade unionism. As we
indicated in Chapter 2, it is very common for latter day UMAs to allow
existing non-members at the time of their introduction to retain that
status and to exempt various other objectors to union membership as
well.

At present, therefore, the extent of rank and file support for the closed
shop must remain conjectural. Since 1979, however, the government has
been determined to ensure that proof of overwhelming support must
exist if closed shops are to retain their legal status. The combined effect
of the 1980 and 1982 Employment Acts will be from November 1984 to
make dismissals for non-membership unfair in any closed shop that has
not been approved by 80 per cent of those covered or 85 per cent of those
voting in a secret ballot within the previous five years. We speculate on
the effects of this legislation in the next chapter. If nothing else, it is likely
to improve our knowledge of rank and file attitudes towards closed
shops.

To What Extent do Closed Shops Result in Employees Reluctantly Joining Trade Unions?

It is impossible to estimate how many people have been forced to join
trade unions because of the operation of the closed shop. Even if we

restrict ourselves to a limited time period, there is no way of quantifying the private feelings and personal decisions of thousands of individuals. How many job applicants would have refused to join a union if it had not been a condition of employment? There is no way of knowing. Indeed many such people would not know themselves. Inertia may have prevented them seeking out a shop steward and asking for a membership form in an open shop. But if a shop steward sought them out they possibly would have joined voluntarily. Or perhaps tightfistedness would have made them take more positive action to avoid the shop steward until, finally cornered, they would be shamed into signing the union form. When does inertia become reluctance? When does informal social pressure become insufficient and contractual obligation decisive? In open shops there are reluctant volunteers just as in closed shops there are enthusiastic conscripts.

So, can any useful calculations be made in relation to reluctant joiners? To some extent it is possible to isolate one group from the mass of people who in the course of their working lives encounter closed shops. These are 'existing non-members' – those who, while not in membership of a union, are faced with the introduction of a closed-shop agreement at their place of work and within a limited period have to choose whether to join the union or lose their job. Their reasons for non-unionism may vary from apathy to meanness to deep moral or religious conviction. But all share that choice. If they decide to take up union membership, they may be crudely classified as reluctant joiners.

How many existing non-members were reluctantly drawn into unions during the 1970s? The first point to make is that generally UMAs were concluded at very high levels of union membership. Table 7.2 shows that in engineering over two-thirds of all closed-shop arrangements emerging between 1965 and 1979 were established when union density was at least 90 per cent. Even so, the table also shows a distinct lowering of the density at which the practice was introduced during the second half of the 1970s as compared to the late 1960s. Indeed it would suggest that by and large the older closed shops developed out of 100 per cent membership and the existing non-member problem is a new phenomenon, a product of the modern UMA. This, however, is an oversimplification. First, we do not know what degree of coercion was used by union members to secure 100 per cent density in the older practices. Was it, for example, achieved through the unilateral imposition of a closed shop which management only recognized once everybody was forced in? Second, the lowering of the density level at which management has been prepared to accept closed-shop agreements was at least

TABLE 7.2   *Union density at the time closed shop introduced by age of arrangement: engineering establishments affiliated to the EEF*

Trade-union density at the time closed-shop arrangement introduced %	Date of closed shop		
	Pre-1965 %	Post-1974 %	All agreements (including 1965–74 UMAs) %.
0	1	3	3
1–49	2	4	5
50–79	9	14	14
80–89	3	16	11
90–94	7	9	10
95–99	11	26	14
100	68	29	42
Proportion introduced at a trade-union density of below 80	11	21	22

Note:
1. All percentages rounded to nearest whole number and so do not total 100.
2. Percentages expressed as a proportion of all closed shops within each category.

partly due to the acceptance by trade unions of liberal UMAs that excluded existing non-members from compulsory unionism. Our estimate that something like two-thirds of UMAs did not force existing non-members into the union (see Chapter 2) hides the true extent of such exemptions in recent years because our sample contained both long-standing agreements, stretching back to the 1960s and beyond, which tended to be tight, and a number of formalizations of 100 per cent arrangements where there were no 'nonners' to exclude. So, the number of reluctant joiners cannot be ascertained merely by looking at the density level at the time of the introduction of the closed shop and by assuming that the difference between this and 100 per cent density is a broad indication of the scale of unwilling recruitment.

Because of the above problems, our estimate of the number of employees compelled to join a union when a closed shop was introduced at their place of work must necessarily be very crude. We put the figure at a quarter of a million during the 1970s (see Table 7.3). As over the same period membership of TUC-affiliated unions increased by 2.9 million, then reluctant joiners accounted for 8 per cent of the growth. We are on rather more certain ground in saying that in some unions the closed shop brought significant membership gains. This was particularly true where the workforce concerned was geographically spread, employed in

TABLE 7.3   *Increases in membership of trade unions as a result of the spread of the closed shop, 1964–80*

% increase in membership from closed-shop agreements and arrangements	Number of unions	Total number of additional members
2% or less	35	45 000
Between 3% and 6%	20	100 000
Between 7% and 10%	16	25 000
Between 11% and 15%	4	70 000
More than 15%	2	20 000
	76	All unions 260 000

small groups, and employed predominantly on a part-time basis. One union – the National Association of Licensed House Managers – which organizes managers in public houses estimated that its membership had increased from 6000 in 1970 to over 16 000 in 1979 as a result of gaining closed-shop arrangements with most of the major brewing companies.

Elsewhere there have been more contentious and well-publicized instances of large numbers being faced with the choice of joining a union or losing their jobs upon the introduction of a full-blooded closed-shop agreement. For example, NALGO officials estimated that the implementation of a closed-shop agreement with the Strathclyde Regional Council increased their membership in that authority from 14 000 to 20 000. Most existing non-unionists with varying degrees of reluctance joined the union but forty-three appealed to the Joint Review Panel which had been established to hear claims from religious objectors. Of these, thirty-four succeeded but of the remaining nine, four joined one of the appropriate unions, one resigned and four were among eleven people whose employment was eventually terminated for refusing to join a union. In 1976 British Rail signed tightened closed-shop agreements with its three major unions and by mid-1976 all but 54 of its 7000 non-unionists at the time of the agreements' introduction had joined the appropriate union. By late 1977 forty non-members who persisted in their objections had been dismissed. In 1980 the Sandwell local authority in the West Midlands introduced a closed shop but of 3500 potential and actual NALGO members to be covered 59 showed a strong reluctance to join. Eventually all but one agreed to join NALGO. There were also difficulties on the introduction in 1976 of an industry-wide closed shop in the footwear industry. In firms where union membership was relatively low there were several incidents and a number of individuals were known to have left employment rather than reluctantly take out union membership. The footwear employers estimated that some 2500 workers reluctantly joined the National Union of Footwear, Leather and Allied Trades (NUFLAT) rather than lose their employment.

However, perhaps the most notorious example of the imposition of the closed shop on unwilling employees was found in the recruitment activities during the 1970s of the former SLADE union among employees in art studios and advertising agencies. The Leggatt Report[8] estimated that by the end of 1979 SLADE had recruited in agencies and studios nearly 8000 employees, the vast majority of whom felt that SLADE was ignorant of their industry, had rules and working practices inappropriate to them and considered the 'join or else your company will be put out of business' method of recruitment scandalous.

To discourage such behaviour, the Conservative government included in the 1980 Employment Act a clause removing the legal immunity from trade unionists who took industrial action to coerce employees of another firm into membership of a particular union. In the 1982 Employment Act two further measures were introduced to try to prevent trade unionists extending unionization to other firms whose employees might have no interest in union membership.[9] The Act made it unlawful to refuse to include firms on tender lists or refuse to offer or award contracts to them on the grounds that they did not employ union members or recognize and negotiate with trade unions. This was aimed especially at a number of local authorities, nationalized industries, and other large, heavily unionized organizations that insisted that subcontractors should employ union members only. The wider, but connected, question of industrial action aimed at preventing an employer fulfilling his contract because not all his employees were members of a trade union was also dealt with by the removal of legal immunities from those who put pressure (e.g. by blacking) upon a non- or semi-unionized contractor to prevent the completion of a contract.[10]

How Frequently does the Closed Shop Result in Individuals Losing Their Employment?

The interview programme covering over 100 major private and public enterprises, seventy-six trade unions together with the postal surveys of EEF-affiliated establishments, certain local authorities and highly

TABLE 7.4 *Estimated minimum number of dismissals of individual workers because of the operation of the closed shop, 1970–81*

Loss of employment due to	Estimated no. of dismissals		
	Pre-entry closed shop	Post-entry closed shop	Total
1. Refusal to join an appropriate trade union on the introduction of a closed shop	10	315	325
2. Failure to gain admission to appropriate trade union	20	74	94
3. Expulsion from appropriate trade union	60	11	71
Total	90	400	490

decentralized private companies covered several million people, establishments and plants and several thousand closed-shop agreements and arrangements. This survey showed that over the period 1970–81 the minimum number of people who lost their job as a result of the operation of the closed shop was 490. (see Table 7.4). This understated the total number of such dismissals because of the relative paucity of information available about dismissals in small firms, some reluctance to respond to questionnaires, and the fact that we were unable to approach all employers with some form of closed-shop arrangement.

Loss of Employment on the Introduction of a Closed Shop

Despite the safeguards mentioned previously provided by collective bargaining, individuals do lose their jobs on the introduction of a closed shop. In fact, 111 instances of such dismissals, which in total involved 325 individuals, were found. The dismissals occurred in thirty companies involved in the survey. Of these ten had only sacked one person and a further twelve either two or three. Nearly 100 of the 325 dismissals were the result of three single incidents. One involved a breakaway union, the second a mass defection of a group of workers from the recognized union and the third occurred when the conscience exemptions from membership were reduced to religious grounds only. The breakdown by industry of the estimated minimum 325 dismissals is shown in Table 7.5. Of this

TABLE 7.5   *Minimum number of dismissals for non-union membership: by industry, 1970–81*

Food, drink and tobacco	6
Engineering	133
Textiles	6
Footwear	8
Other manufacturing	26
Retail distribution	60
Local government	18
Railways	54
Electricity supply	6
Entertainment industry	8
Total	325

total a handful were individuals dismissed before 1974 or after 1980. the remainder were dismissed in the 1974–80 period.

While proponents of the closed shop may argue that an estimated minimum 325 dismissals is a relatively small number compared with the total population covered by closed shops, critics would see the figure as substantial arguing that one dismissal is one too many. To increase individual protection, the Employment Act 1980 sought to give statutory redress to existing non-uionists on the introduction of a closed shop by making it automatically unfair to dismiss a non-union employee in such circumstances. At the same time the Act extended the right to non-union membership in a closed shop where an employee could show a genuine objection to trade-union membership on grounds of conscience or other deeply held personal conviction. The government later decided that these measures were insufficient since they provided no redress for existing non-unionists who had lost their jobs for refusing to join a union on the introduction of a closed shops between 1974 and 1980. It also considered that the changes in unfair dismissal legislation introduced in 1974 and 1976 relating to the non-union membership in closed shops were arbitrary, oppressive and morally indefensible in that people with conscientious objections to union membership were dismissed from employment without redress.[11] The Employment Act 1982 made compensation available to anyone so dismissed between 1974 and 1980 provided they already held the job before the closed shop was introduced or had a genuine conscientious objection to belonging to a trade union. The Act made a total sum of £2 million available to provide such compensation payments.

The government estimated that the number involved was approximately 400.[12] Compensation was calculated according to what an industrial tribunal would have awarded at the time if the dismissal had been unfair, together with interest. Account was also taken of the actual loss suffered as a result of time subsequently spent out of work. Cases were referred to an independent assessor who advised the Secretary of State for Employment both on the individual's eligibility for compensation and on the amount to be paid.[13] These 'retrospective' compensation provisions of the 1982 Act came into being on 1 November 1982 and individuals who considered themselves eligible had to have made a claim by 1 November 1983. By the end of February 1983 380 people had applied for compensation and the Department of Employment was still receiving applications.[14]

Table 7.6 shows the occupational breakdown of these 380. The Department announced the first awards in December 1982 when payments of £284, £1552 and £10 778 were made. The highest payment went to an individual dismissed in September 1977, after thirty-one years' service in an engineering company, for refusing to join the AUEW on the introduction of a closed shop.[15]

In early 1981 the issue of dismissal from employment on the introduction of a closed shop again became a matter of public debate following incidents at two local authorities in the West Midlands. In 1980 the Sandwell Metropolitan District Council signed a closed-shop agreement with its non-manual unions but in February 1981 Miss Joanna Harris was dismissed from employment when she refused to take out union membership. Although her plight was taken up by the Freedom Association she failed to regain her job. A few months later the Walsall Metropolitan District Council, under a new closed-shop arrangement, dismissed four part-time school dinner ladies. They took their cases to a tribunal and were found to have been unfairly dismissed by virtue of the protections established by the 1980 Employment Act. The tribunal ordered their reinstatement but the employer refused to comply with the order. Subsequently the four received financial compensation totalling £10 598.[16]

The public concern surrounding the events of the Sandwell and Walsall councils led the government to conclude that the existing levels of compensation available to those dismissed because of the closed shop did not act as a sufficient deterrent to an employer who was of a mind to dismiss an employee unfairly in order to enforce a closed-shop agreement. The Employment Act 1982 therefore increased substantially the level of compensation available in such cases. The Act also provided that anyone so treated because of trade-union pressure should be able to seek compensation directly from that union.

TABLE 7.6 Applications for 'retrospective' compensation under section 2 of the Employment Act 1982 as at end of February 1983

Occupational group	Date not stated	1972	1973	1974	1975	1976	1977	1978	1979	1980	1981	1982	All
Managerial (general management)	—	—	—	—	—	—	—	—	—	—	—	—	—
Professional and related supporting management and administration	—	—	—	—	—	—	—	1	1	—	—	—	2
Professional and related in education, welfare and health	—	—	—	—	—	—	1	1	2	—	—	—	4
Literature, artistic, sports	—	—	—	—	2	—	1	—	—	1	—	—	4
Professional and related in science, engineering, technology and similar fields	1	—	—	—	2	4	—	—	1	3	1	—	13

Occupation													Total
Managerial (ex-general management)	—	—	—	—	—	1	2	1	2	—	—	—	6
Clerical and related	2	—	—	2	20	11	3	4	3	—	—	—	45
Selling	1	—	—	—	—	11	1	—	1	—	—	—	14
Security, protective service	1	—	—	—	—	1	2	1	1	—	—	—	6
Catering, cleaning, hairdressing and other personal service	2	—	—	1	5	2	4	2	3	1	—	—	20
Farming, fishing and related	—	—	—	—	—	—	2	—	—	—	—	—	2
Material processing	1	—	—	1	5	8	3	8	3	3	—	3	35
Making and repairing	2	—	—	—	3	4	2	1	2	2	—	1	17
Processing, making, repairing and related	3	—	—	2	11	16	17	11	7	9	—	—	76
Painting, repetitive, assembling, product inspection, packaging and related	3	—	—	3	7	6	10	8	5	1	—	1	44
Construction, mining and related not identified elsewhere	1	1	—	—	3	1	1	1	1	5	1	—	15
Transport operations, materials, moving and storing	5	—	—	4	3	15	12	5	7	2	1	1	55
Miscellaneous	3	—	—	—	3	3	3	3	1	—	—	—	16
Occupation not stated	4	—	—	—	1	1	—	—	—	—	—	—	6
All occupations	28	1	—	13	39	83	85	44	45	34	2	6	380

A further event that strengthened the case of those favouring legislation against the closed shop came in the wake of the British Railways Board's mass dismissal of employees after 1976 for their refusal to join the appropriate trade union on the tightening of the railway closed-shop agreements. Three railwaymen took their case to the European Commission on Human Rights which in December 1979, by a majority of fourteen to three, upheld their claim that their dismissal for refusing to join a trade union in a closed shop violated the European Human Rights Convention. The grounds of the Commission's ruling were unexpected. The three applicants contended that their dismissal for refusing to join a union infringed their rights under article 11(i) of the Convention which guaranteed the individual the right to freedom of association with others including the right to form and to join trade unions for the protection of their interests. They claimed that such a right implied the negative right to dissociate. The Commission declined to consider this point or to give their opinions on the closed shop in general. Instead the Commission concentrated on the issue that the three men were required to join one of the named unions in the agreement with no option to join another union of their choice or form their own union. The Commission emphasized that article 11(i) gave individuals the right to join trade unions in the plural, thus excluding a monopoly of a particular union or unions. The Commission found that the compulsion on them to join specific unions was an interference with their freedom to join or set up a union of their choice.

The complainants however were not objecting to being prevented from joining the union of their choice but to joining any union at all. In addition, two of the three objected to trade-union policies and activities while one also objected to the political affiliations of the three railway unions. The judgement had more meaning in terms of European industrial relations where closed shops are less common and where the divisions between unions are often on political and religious grounds. In these circumstances workers might well have a ideological reason for not wanting to join a particular union.

The Commission referred the case in May 1980 to the European Court of Human Rights which handed down its judgement in August 1981. The Court said that it was not necessary to decide whether the 'right to associate' also implied the 'negative right' not to join a union and the closed-shop system as such was not being reviewed. In addition the judgement stated it was unnecessary to express an opinion on every consequence of compulsion that a closed shop might engender. However, by a majority of eight to three the Court ruled that the railways' closed shop in compelling the three individuals to join a union or lose their employment 'struck at the very heart of freedoms' guaranteed by the European Convention on Human Rights. The Court based its findings heavily on two facts. First, all the three former railwaymen had been existing employees when the closed shop was introduced, and second, two of the three had alleged conscientious objections to union membership. The Court confined its adjudication to the particular case and did not rule that there should be an outright ban on the closed shop. Both supporters and opponents of compulsory unionism could claim comfort from the railway case although it did appear to show that between 1976 and 1980 the legislation on dismissals for non-union membership may have contravened the European Convention on Human Rights. Certainly the case was a factor in the government's decision in 1982 to provide retrospective compensation for those legally dismissed during that period.

Loss of Employment or Job Opportunities through
Failure to Gain Admission to the Appropriate Trade Union

Where closed shops exist an individual's failure to obtain a union card means that he cannot secure a job within it. In such circumstances trade-union rules on admission become particularly crucial. For that reason we surveyed trade-union regulations on admission through an examination of the rule books as at 1979 of seventy-nine unions with a total membership of 12 million. Most, if not all, operated closed shops. The main findings of our survey have been reported elsewhere.[17] All unions mentioned some form of entry requirement in their rule books, although they varied considerably in detail, the craft unions being most precise. Few provided for notification of the reason for rejection of applications and even fewer provided rejected applicants with a right of appeal.

However, the importance of formal rules can be exaggerated and consideration needs to be given to how they are applied in practice. The vagueness of admission rules can be partly attributed to the paucity of problems that arise in admitting people to unions, particularly where post-entry closed shops operate. Moreover, unions usually issue hand-books providing guidance to shop stewards, branch and full-time officials on the application of such rules and procedures. These guide-lines effectively extend the rights of individuals beyond those formally specified in the rule books. Nevertheless failures to obtain jobs and dismissals do occur (see Table 7.4). In the case of post-entry closed shops such instances are rare. Unions who are party to post-entry arrangements tend to want the additional members. Certainly management did not see this as a recruiting problem. The principal difficulty arises when people previously in union membership apply to transfer to the union *in situ* upon starting work in a closed shop and fall foul of the 'Bridlington Principles' which operate among unions affiliated to the TUC.[18] Our research showed that under the Principles the main reason for refusing to admit an applicant seeking entry to a post-entry shop was arrears of contributions to their previous union. Sometimes this was due to maladministration by the union at local level. Apart from Bridlington, refusal of admission was also justified on the grounds that: the individual had previously resigned membership to avoid participation in industrial action; existing members objected; fraud had allegedly occurred; the applicant had failed to give an assurance that he would abide by the rules and policies of the union. None was common. Only twenty-five instances, involving a total of seventy-four people, were discovered of employees being unable to take up a job or to continue in a job because union membership was withheld where a post-entry shop operated.

The pre-entry closed shop is very different. Its *raison d'être* is to exclude people from jobs by denying them union membership – hence the detailed admission rules in many craft union rule books relating to, for example, apprenticeships. It would be impossible to estimate how many people have been excluded from jobs because they failed to meet the unions' criteria. For example, how many potentially competent actors have abandoned their profession because of the difficulty of obtaining an Equity card? How many semi-skilled workers capable of being trained to perform skilled tasks have not been given the opportunity to do so because at 16 they chose not to undertake an apprenticeship? Such questions raise all kinds of issues about labour market restrictions and job opportunities. How many potentially brilliant barristers missed their vocation because they could not merely walk into a courtroom with a wig and a gown but first had to undergo an expensive training at an Inn of Court which they could not afford or could not secure? Professional qualifications like trade-union pre-entry qualifications are subject to all kinds of rules that have varying degrees of relevance to the jobs involved but that serve to protect those qualified by limiting entry to them. Few make a concerted effort to challenge the prevailing restrictions because the obstacles seem insurmountable. Unfulfilled ambitions remain hidden.

However, it is possible to make some estimate of those who, though appropriately qualified according to union regulations, have nevertheless been debarred from union membership where pre-entry shops operate. Even though a few extreme cases have attracted publicity,[19] the incidence is low. We identified twenty in recent years. The most common reason was that the appropriately qualified individual had not been offered a job by the relevant employer. A second was that the union branch concerned had unemployed members on its list and felt that these should have the first call on any employment offers. Generally the latitude with which many pre-entry unions exercise their exclusion powers where appropriately qualified people are concerned leads to little friction. Weekes *et al.*'s exploration of the effects of the 1971 Industrial Relations Act, for example, found very few cases relating to its provision that any person who applied for membership of a union and was appropriately qualified to do the work in the area covered by the union should not be arbitrarily or unreasonably excluded from membership.[20]

Latterly, however, craft unions have been criticized not so much for their handling of appropriately qualified workers, but more for their defence of the qualifications themselves which often in centring on apprenticeship training have become outmoded by new technology. Yet, as we saw in Chapter 3, such unions are beginning to change their criteria for membership as they seek to establish control over the latest production techniques. In 1974, for example, the NGA added a third category of workers it was prepared to accept, namely 'anybody it was in the best interests of the Association to admit'. Another union official told us that whereas twenty years previously only time-served craftsmen could obtain a union card, nowadays successful completion of an IBM computer course was often sufficient.

To sum up, although formal trade-union rules may support the view that the interests of the individual are not properly safeguarded, the actual operation of these rules does not generally carry potential abuses into practice. Consequently the statutory safeguards provided by the 1982 Employment Act to protect individuals from arbitrary or unreasonable exclusion from union membership in a closed shop may be as little used as their 1971 predecessors.

Loss of Employment Through Expulsion from a Trade Union

Our survey of union expulsion rules revealed that they are open to many of the criticisms levelled at admission regulations. Indeed many of these criticisms were raised by the Donovan Commission in the 1960s. Frequently unions rely on general or 'blanket' clauses in imposing discipline rather than specifying certain offences. In addition the principles of natural justice tend not to be explicitly mentioned.

Procedural rights for members accused of misdemeanors are often not spelt out in detail. Yet, as with admissions, the shortcomings of the formal rules do not necessarily mean that in practice members receive arbitrary or unfair treatment. Again guidelines are provided to flesh out the barebones of the rule book. These usually establish or improve procedural rights for protecting individuals although not always to the standards of natural justice.

A further line of defence, however, is contained in those UMAs that set out a method by which the union keeps management informed of the progress of discipline and expulsion cases. The scope for jointly agreed procedures in this area is somewhat limited by unions' reluctance to compromise the autonomy of their internal disciplinary machinery. Yet many UMAs give management the right to explore the merits of any case involved and discuss their implications in relation to possible dismissals. As was shown in Chapter 2, it has become common for signatory unions to accept that the final appeals body in expulsion disputes is the TUC's Independent Review Committee, the work of which is discussed later. In general, employers reported few difficulties arising from union disciplinary procedures. Seldom did instances occur where their own rights under UMAs had to be invoked.

Recent systematic evidence on the extent and nature of union disciplinary activities is lacking. During the 1960s, however, a survey conducted for the Donovan Commission by the Government Social Survey Unit[21] questioned 494 trade unionists concerning the disciplining of union members by the union itself or by fellow members at the workplace. Eleven per cent reported such cases, although only 4 per cent of these considered that the disciplining had been unfair. In none of these 'unfair' incidents did expulsion occur. Follow-up questions were asked about appeals against disciplinary decisions. Seven were reported, one of which was considered unfair.[22] This survey was not of course confined to closed-shop areas and its age may make it of limited utility in the present-day debate. Clearly, further research is needed. Our own discussions with over eighty senior full-time union officials revealed seven instances of at least one member being disciplined for a specific or general offence and subsequently being dismissed because of the closed shop. The number of people involved was sixty.

The majority of expulsions in closed-shop contexts were the result of members falling into arrears. Such instances were nevertheless unusual, not least because of the spread of 'check-off'. The majority of UMAs signed in the 1970s were accompanied by or preceded by the introduction of check-off. Moreover, very few people expelled for arrears lost their jobs, since the main reason for lapsing was that the lapsee had moved out of the area of compulsory union membership. Where people fell out of compliance within closed shops, unions tended to approach the problem flexibly, allowing people to remain in membership for a considerably longer period than the rule book stated before moving to expel them. Eventual expulsion was often followed by an application to rejoin and readmission was seldom withheld, although the applicant returned as a new member, losing previously accrued benefit rights. Even so, rigidity sometimes led to dismissals. A SOGAT member, for example, working in a pre-entry shop, authorized his employer to deduct his union dues from his wage packet. Due to an administrative error by the union, his authorization was not implemented. He fell into arrears, was expelled from the union and lost his job. Unable to find another in the printing industry, he took legal action against SOGAT for wrongful expulsion. The court found in his favour and he was readmitted.

Of more significance to industrial relations is the use of expulsion for failure to answer a strike call with subsequent forfeiture of job. Apart from the baking industry dispute of 1978, no major instances of expulsion in such circumstances were encountered, although of 450 expulsions reported to us by union officials, 275 related to isolated industrial dispute offences, not necessarily in closed shops. In most cases the individuals concerned were eventually readmitted to the union. A major reason for the reluctance of unions to punish strike breakers in this way was graphically illustrated by the baking dispute. It involved 26 000 members of the bakers' union, of whom 2000 refused to participate in the stoppage. Delegates to a special union conference voted to expel them. The Bakers' Federation, the employers' association, responded by confirming its intention to terminate the existing industry-wide post-entry closed-shop agreement and by stating that its member firms would continue to employ the expelled members.

In the face of such a large-scale revolt, use of the expulsion weapon would appear to involve great risk to the union in terms of reduced subscription revenue, discontented members and ex-members, vulnerability to poaching by other unions, and loss of face. Unions frequently prefer to take milder disciplinary action – such as imposing fines or withdrawing membership rights – against those who do not answer strike calls or who return to work prematurely. Yet difficulties can still arise in closed shops if the disciplined members challenge the penalties imposed on them, as happened on the railways in early 1983. In June 1982 the National Union of Railwaymen called an official strike over pay. However, 12 500 members continued to work and eventually the union was forced to call off the strike and to seek arbitration. Disciplinary proceedings were instigated and in October 1982 the union announced that all those who defied the strike instruction would be deprived of non-cash benefits (e.g. legal assistance) for five years and barred from holding union office for the same period. Existing local officials who had opted to work through the strike were permanently removed from union office.[23] A disciplined member from Derby reacted to these penalties by resigning from the NUR and in January 1983 200 fellow workers decided to follow his example in protest at the 'harsh' punishment meted out to non-strikers, even though they themselves had participated in the industrial action.[24] Indeed, two resigning members from Derby formed a breakaway union – the Federation of Railway Workers – as NUR members in Crewe, Swindon, Reading and York began to defect from the NUR. To an extent this was a consequence of the British Rail Chairman's pledge made at the time of the stoppage that no employee expelled for not striking would be sacked in accordance with the closed-shop agreement. But perhaps the ramifications were unforeseen by management. Issuing the guarantee to expelled strike breakers was a limited sanction against the union during the dispute. Indeed the Chairman had stated that the British Railways Board intended the closed-shop agreement to continue. Offering the same guarantee to non-strikers who resigned and then to strikers who resigned in sympathy with them was likely to place the closed shop in more permanent jeopardy.

Such problems place both unions and management in a considerable dilemma. To avoid them, a method of dealing with members who disregard strike calls or return to work before a strike is over has evolved in printing. During the 1959 six-week strike in the general printing and provincial newspaper industry, the Typographical Association (now a constituent part of the NGA) advised the expulsion of all strike breakers, a severe punishment in a trade dominated by pre-entry practices. However, under the terms of settlement the union side agreed to 'withdraw or refrain from any punitive action or discrimination against employers or employees in respect of their actions or activities during the dispute or stoppage of work' in return for an employer undertaking not to victimize union members involved in the industrial action. This formula, devised with the help of Lord Burkitt, who had been appointed to assist the two sides settle their differences, came to be interpreted as giving the union the right to discipline within its rules short of permanent expulsion. For example, the union could impose a fine on expelled strike breakers in the form of a re-entrance fee and they would lose their accrued membership benefits.

In August 1959 the union instructed its branches to approach those expelled during the dispute and to offer them the opportunity to make a new application for membership. However, the formula ran into difficulties at the *Leicester Mercury* where the strike had not been fully effective. The company refused to re-engage over 100 strikers since they considered that the union intended to take punitive action against employees who had remained at work. It claimed that depriving readmitted members of their continuity of membership rights was an excessive punishment.[25] The matter was referred to Lord Burkitt who advised the union to rescind its decision to strip strike breakers of their accrued benefits and to substitute a reasonable fine to mark their disapproval of breaches of union rules and discipline. In November 1959 the Typographical Association decided that all expelled members, numbering about 500, should be accepted into the union again upon payment of £20.

This basis for dealing with strike breakers was used again by the NGA in the case of thirty-three machine managers who returned to work during *The Times* dispute of 1979. The Burkitt Formula was applied and they were asked to pay a re-entry fee of £70 which was considered to be the equivalent of the £20 levied in 1959. However, unlike in 1959 the machine managers were accepted only as new members. It was felt that the loss of benefits involved did not have the same significance as it did to Typographical Association members twenty years earlier. The fines were paid and membership restored. The NGA also employed the Burkitt Formula in disciplining members who returned to work during the 1980 general printing and provincial newspaper dispute and the Formula has been adopted by other print unions operating pre-entry shops.

To What Extent Does the Closed Shop Cause Individuals to Participate Reluctantly in Industrial Action?

In theory the value of the closed shop to trade unions as a means to secure strike solidarity lies not so much in the *ex-post facto* expulsion of strike breakers, although this might of course have a deterrent effect in the future, but in the threat of such action causing reluctant members to obey the strike call. Thus the effect of the closed shop on strike activity cannot be measured merely in terms of the volume of expulsions and resultant dismissals in the aftermath of strikes. It must be measured in terms of the extent to which members who do not wish to strike decide to do so because they fear the consequences of staying at work in terms of eventual job loss. Although the evidence presented in this and the previous chapter might suggest that, given perfect knowledge, members would judge their chances of being dismissed through the operation of the closed shop as slim, we cannot assume such perfect knowledge. In the uncertainty and emotion of an industrial dispute the threat might seem very real. However, in determining the decisiveness of this threat in cajoling people into strike action, we encounter the familiar problem of disentangling the impact of the closed shop from all kinds of factors that determine workers' behaviour at critical junctures. In all strikes there is likely to be a proportion, sometimes quite a high proportion, of workers who are less than enthusiastic about withdrawing their labour. For some it might be a matter of principle or loyalty to the company, for others calculation that the strike cannot achieve anything, for others a calculation that the financial costs will be too great, and for yet others a fear of managerial retribution. In a closed shop, their reluctant participation in the strike may be the result of a greater fear of union retribution. But there may be more immediate pressures that overcome the individual's doubts: feelings of solidarity overriding financial considerations; a desire to conform with fellow workers' actions prevailing over company loyalty; a sense of injustice outweighing misgivings about the strike's chances of success; fear of the disapproval of workmates and being branded a 'blackleg'. Given such a complex interplay of pressures upon individuals when a strike occurs, we find it difficult to reach any firm conclusion about the effectiveness of the closed-shop threat. It is nevertheless fairly certain that the closed shop cannot turn a workforce that does not want to strike into one that is capable of sustaining effective strike action. This was certainly management's view. Even so, the closed shop may have a marginal effect in persuading small pockets of reluctant strikers to withdraw their labour.

Voluntary and Statutory Protection for Individuals against Unreasonable Exclusion or Expulsion from Trade Unions where Closed Shops Exist

In recent years public concern about the potential power of trade unions over individuals through arbitrary use of exclusion and expulsion in closed-shop contexts has led to demands for statutory protection against such acts. The trade-union movement has sought to ward off such legislation by introducing measures designed to allay criticism arising from the operation of the practice. These have included the TUC issuing model rules on admission and expulsion from unions, the establishment of the TUC Independent Review Committee, and the publication of a TUC guide on how closed shops should be introduced and operated.

In June 1969, following the Donovan Report, the TUC published its own proposals for the reform of the internal rules and procedures of affiliated unions.[26] Ten years later our survey of union rule books showed that few unions had altered their rules on admission and expulsion in the light of these recommendations or as a result of more members being drawn into closed shops. Only the General and Municipal Workers, the Agricultural Workers and the Fire Brigades Union made significant changes. For example, the FBU discussed how its disciplinary rules should be amended to accommodate its policy of seeking UMAs with local authorities. The final stage of the union's existing appeals was the annual conference which often meant lengthy delays between the initial decision to expel and the final settlement of the case. The union decided that a new final appeals body consisting of regional officers should be set up to speed up the process.

A more significant reform has been the TUC Independent Review Committee (IRC), constituted in 1976 to consider appeals from individuals dismissed or given notice of dismissal from their jobs as a result of exclusion or expulsion from a union where membership was a condition of employment.[27] Although the Committee was established under the auspices of the TUC, it was intended to be independent in making decisions. Its members are appointed in consultation with the Secretary of State for Employment and the Chairman of ACAS. Before considering an appeal the Committee must be satisfied that the complainant has exhausted all internal union procedures. If this condition has been met, the Committee discusses the case with the union and the person concerned and tries to resolve the matter by conciliating between them. If agreement cannot be reached, it makes a recommendation on whether the admission or readmission should take place and on what conditions. After reaching this decision, the Committee has often found it useful to adopt a process known as 'post-hearing conciliation'. This is undertaken only with the agreement of the parties and its objective is to explore the possibilities of finding an agreed method to help the complaint find a way back into employment. The union concerned is expected to act upon any recommendation.[28]

Our research showed that generally unions refusing admission to or expelling an individual have brought the existence of the IRC to his attention, even though few unions have written the Committee into their rules. Moreover, a significant number of UMAs have stipulated it as the final level of appeal available to those in difficulties with their union membership. Even so, the Committee's case load has not been heavy. Between April 1976 and June 1983 it received forty-nine complaints. Of these, twenty-one involving forty-four people, went to the formal hearing stage. Seventeen complaints, encompassing twenty individuals, were rejected as being outside the Committee's terms of references.[29] Six cases, covering twenty-four people, involved the refusal of a union to admit non-unionists into membership, while seven instances, each involving one individual, concerned a refusal to admit workers who had previously been members of other unions. In the remaining eight cases, involving thirteen people, the complaint related to unfair expulsion from a trade union with resultant loss of job. As regards the outcome of these cases, in ten, involving seventeen individuals, the Committee recommended that the union should admit or readmit the complainants into membership. All the unions concerned implemented these decisions. In a further six cases, where twenty-two workers were involved, the Committee decided that the unions should give sympathetic consideration to admitting or readmitting the complaints. Again the unions complied with the Committee's wishes. In the remaining five cases, the IRC felt it could make to recommendation.

The effectiveness of the IRC in protecting individuals from arbitrary or unreasonable exclusion or expulsion from trade unions where closed shops exist has been questioned. It has no power to compel admission or readmission and cannot award compensation to a wronged individual, nor require the attendance of witnesses, nor insist upon the production of documents, nor take evidence from the employer concerned. Adverse comment has also been made on the fact that, since the Committee cannot consider a case until all internal union procedures have been exhausted, a long time may elapse between the action about which the individual is complaining and the final appeal to the IRC.[30] However, the most severe criticism has been that in no instance has the complaint regained his job after taking his case to the Committee, even though after six hearings, concerning thirteen people, the recommendation was that the union should help appellants back into employment.

Perhaps the outcome of six cases is insufficient evidence to make a final judgement on the IRC's ability to secure the re-employment of complainants. To date, at least part of the problem has been the limited power of the trade unions to force employers to reinstate or re-engage workers dismissed in such circumstances, especially at a time of economic recession. For example, in four of the cases handled by the IRC the employers refused to re-employ eleven people because they were not currently recruiting labour. Evidence also suggests that a statutory tribunal might not offer much greater prospects of success in achieving re-engagement. In 1977, for instance, 72 per cent of those claiming unfair dismissal sought the remedy of reinstatement or re-engagement from the Industrial Tribunal, yet only 5 per cent of successful claimants obtained such a remedy.[31] On the other hand, Lewis has suggested that these figures give a misleading impression. He has produced evidence to show that, while most applicants want their jobs back at the time of their application to the Tribunal, by the time the hearing takes place they prefer financial compensation. He concluded that the majority of applicants to Industrial Tribunals who succeed in the unfair dismissal obtain the remedy they seek.[32] Moreover, the advantage to the individual of a statutory procedure to deal with cases of unreasonable exclusion or expulsion from trade unions in closed-shop contexts would be that, even if it were not the preferred remedy, financial compensation would be available to those who lost their jobs, and would penalize unions who acted arbitrarily, perhaps persuading them to alter their subsequent behaviour. In addition a statutory procedure would possibly prevent dismissals taking place by allowing cases of unreasonable expulsion to be brought before dismissal occurs, whereas the IRC can only consider problems where dismissal has taken place or notice of dismissal issued. In such circumstances a Tribunal's declaration of unreasonable expulsion would put pressure upon the union to readmit the individual or at least not to press the employer to dismiss him.

While accepting some of the limitations of the IRC in protecting individuals in admission or expulsion difficulties, it must be said that this voluntary machinery has had the advantage of enjoying the goodwill of the TUC unions which has contributed to its success rate in securing the admittance and readmittance of complainants. It has also allowed the Committee to adopt a flexible approach to the problems before it. For example, where it has proved impractical to readmit a former member to his previous branch, the Committee has recommended that another branch should take him. Where for industrial-relations reasons it has seemed imprudent to insist that a complainant be given back his old job, it has recommended that an alternative workplace should be found.[33] In short, the IRC has tended to seek practical solutions balancing the interests of the individual, the union and the company and taking into consideration the industrial-relations implications involved.

The limitations of the IRC were nevertheless a factor in the

Conservative government's decision in 1979 to introduce statutory protection for people excluded or expelled from unions where closed shops operated. Under the 1980 Employment Act any person employed or seeking employment in a job where it was the practice to require membership of a trade union was given the right not to have an application for membership unreasonably refused and the right not to be unreasonably expelled from the union. Complaints were to be presented to an industrial tribunal which was to decide whether the exclusion or expulsion was reasonable or not in accordance with equity and the substantial merits of the case, not merely in accordance with the union's rule book. If the union found the complaint justified, it was to make a declaration that the exclusion or expulsion was unreasonable. Where such a declaration was made by the tribunal, or on appeal by the Employment Appeals Tribunal, the person involved could apply for compensation from the union for any loss suffered.

The statutory protection was strengthened by the 1982 Employment Act. This stipulated that the dismissal of an employee for non-union membership under a closed shop was unfair where the employee concerned had obtained a declaration of unreasonable exclusion or expulsion from the union under the 1980 Act and where he had an application for such a declaration pending. The intention was that, in tandem with the substantially enhanced levels of compensation for all unfair closed-shop dismissals contained in the 1982 Act, this protection would increase the individual's chances of retaining or regaining his job.

In reaching decisions on the reasonableness of exclusions or expulsions, Tribunals must take into consideration the *Code of Practice on Closed Shop Agreements and Arrangements*.[34] On admission to membership the Code indicates the need for clear and fair rules and the factors that trade unions should take into account when considering applications; for example, the qualifications of the applicant, and whether the number of applicants or potential applicants is likely to be so great as to pose a serious threat of undermining negotiated terms and conditions of employment. On expulsions, the *Code* stresses that in general voluntary procedures are preferable to statutory, but it advises that unions should not discipline members whose refusal to take industrial action was because the action as unlawful; in breach of a statutory duty or the criminal law, constituted a serious risk to public safety, health or property; was in breach of a procedural agreement; had not been approved in a secret ballot; or contravened their professional or other code of ethics.

By summer 1983 little use had been made of the above legislation. The ACAS *Annual Report 1981* noted that out of 48 000 individual conciliation cases it dealt with during that year only sixteen concerned alleged unreasonable expulsion or exclusion from a trade union where membership was compulsory.[35] Conciliation was continuing at the end of 1981 in nine of these sixteen cases. Of the other seven, two were withdrawn and five went to Tribunals that found in favour of the claimant. Appeals were made against these decisions and the Employment Appeals Tribunal eventually overturned them.

8 The Closed Shop in 1980s: Conclusions and Prospects

INTRODUCTION

Our research has focused on the development of the closed shop in the two decades since McCarthy's study. In drawing together the strands of this research, is it possible to ascertain how the closed shop will fare in the 1980s? From recent happenings the decade would appear to be one of considerable uncertainty for the practice. The period of growth as a result of which the closed-shop population reached a peak in the late 1970s seemed to be ending in 1979, even before a Conservative government was elected and passed legislation that presented significant obstacles to further expansion. Is further growth still possible in the 1980s? After all, even at its peak the practice covered less than half of all trade-union members. Or did the period from the late 1960s to the late 1970s bring together a combination of factors favourable to the closed shop's spread which are unlikely to be repeated in the 1980s? And what of existing closed shops? Are they durable enough to survive the harsher legal and economic climates of the present decade? Will the closed shop decline significantly? Will it fade from industrial relations altogether?[1] To tackle these questions we begin by briefly isolating the factors we consider salient to the recent growth of the closed shop.

First, by the 1960s the British trade-union movement was undoubtedly closed shop prone. Because they lacked positive rights under the abstentionist system of labour law, trade unionists had learnt collective self-reliance in protecting their interests. In the industries where trade unions had had most impact, this had included a willingness to compel fellow workers into the union or to exclude them from the job, methods that had secured legal toleration, not least because abstentionism offered individual workers no right to dissociate. As the 1960s arrived, in excess of 40 per cent of trade unionists were covered by closed-shop arrangements. The remainder may have lacked the motivation or

145

have been too weak to impose the practice on generally hostile employers. Nevertheless, the closed-shop tradition was deeply embedded in unionists' consciousness and folklore.

Second, the conditions that translated this closed shop proneness into a surge of activity to secure the practice had clearly emerged by the late 1960s. Overt signs of a deep-seated economic malaise, following the long period of post-war prosperity, stimulated both trade-union growth and trade-union interest in the closed shop. This meshed with a growing management interest in the practice. To counter powerful shop-floor trade unionism built up over a long period, management sought to involve union representatives on detailed formal regulation of the workplace, and saw compulsory unionism as an aid to their joint influence over the workforce. The result was an initial boost of closed-shop agreements at the turn of the decade.

Third, although legislative obstacles blocked this activity in the early 1970s, after 1974 the reintroduction of a permissive legal framework allowed its resumption. Gathering momentum, it becomes less associated with the search for more effective joint regulation, and more a ritual endorsement of such reforms.

THE 1980s

We now apply the four interlocking variables – economic forces, legislation, management and trade-union attitudes – to the 1980s.

From the late 1970s, economic deterioration became far more marked. From mid-1978 to mid-1982 the number of unemployed on an unadjusted seasonal basis increased from 1.4 million to 3.2 million – a rise of nearly 130 per cent. To varying degrees it hit almost all industries as the total workforce fell from 22.2 million to 20 million, a reduction of nearly 10 per cent. Worst affected was manufacturing. In metal manufacture employment fell by 35 per cent; in textiles by 30 per cent; in vehicles and mechanical engineering by 25 per cent; in shipbuilding by 21 per cent; and clothing and footwear by 21 per cent. One effect was the first significant decline in trade-union membership since the 1920s. TUC affiliated membership dwindled from a peak of 12.2 million in 1979 to approximately 11 million in 1981. As many of these industries were extensively covered by closed-shop arrangements, it is safe to say that the closed-shop population was also affected. If we assume that closed-shop growth has been insignificant in the 1980s, that existing closed-shop areas have not become 'open', and that the decline in employment was

TABLE 8.1   *Estimates of extent of closed shop at mid-1982*

Industry	No. of employees in employment (000s) mid-1982	Estimated no. of employees in closed shops (000s) mid-1982	Fall in no. relative to mid-1978 (000s)
Agriculture, forestry and fishing	341	3	Nil
Mining and quarrying	324	282	−14
Food, drink and tobacco	586	223	−43
Coal and petroleum	33	18	− 2
Chemical and allied industries	376	120	−17
Metal manufacture	299	150	−78
Mechanical engineering	695	313	−99
Instrument engineering	120	12	− 4
Electrical engineering	612	184	−36
Shipbuilding and marine engineering	139	79	−20
Vehicles	570	274	−95
Metal goods not elsewhere classified	407	134	−44
Textiles	328	69	−31
Leather, leather goods and fur	29	4	− 2
Clothing and footwear	287	66	−17
Bricks, pottery, glass, cement. etc.	201	66	−22
Timber and furniture	211	61	−15
Paper, printing and publishing	473	312	−42
Other manufacturing industries	245	100	−37
Construction	992	69	−20
Gas, electricity and water	322	258	−15
Transport and communications	1 363	763	−35
Distributive trades	2 518	378	−19
Insurance, banking, finance and business service	1 203	60	+ 8

evenly distributed across occupational groups, then we can calculate that the closed-shop population had been eroded by unemployment from a 5.2 million minimum in 1978 to approximately 4.5 million by 1982, a drop of 13 per cent (see Table 8.1). This is a higher proportionate drop than that of trade-union membership generally and than that of the total workforce. As the 1980s progress, quite apart from the impact of any further unemployment, how safe will it be to presume (i) that the decline in the closed-shop population will not be offset by the appearance of new arrangements, or (ii) that it will not be steepened by the dismantling or lapsing of existing practices?.

Possibilities of the Spread of the Closed Shop to New Areas in the 1980s

The slowing of closed-shop activity in the late 1970s was dramatic. Of well over 2000 formal closed-shop agreements recorded during our research, 33 per cent were concluded in 1978 and only 5 per cent in 1979 and 2 per cent in the first half of 1980. From this we conclude that by 1980 compulsory unionism had come to exist in most areas where conditions were conducive to it. The areas where conditions were not conducive could be divided into three.

The first was characterized by strong managerial resistance to union demands for the practice, as in the Civil Service, the wool textile industry, the hosiery and knitwear industry, parts of construction, the local authorities, and the health service, and journalism.[2] Resistance was based both on principle and on a feeling that the closed shop would interfere with important organizational goals. For example, employers in wool textiles and in Conservative-controlled local authorities felt it was an unacceptable infringement of individual liberty. Central government, irrespective of the political party in power, opposed compulsory unionism on the grounds that it might be used by the unions to politicize the Civil Service. Provincial newspaper proprietors felt that it would conflict with editorial freedom to decide the content of their publications. We feel confident that, if anything, economic conditions are likely to bolster employer opposition in the 1980s and that the unions are unlikely to be able to muster enough support to overcome it, especially as the 1980 Act required massive popular support before a new closed shop became legally defensible. Indeed, available evidence suggests that, confronted with more pressing matters of concern to their members, the unions have ceased to accord the closed shop a high priority.

The second area was characterized by high union density yet little demand for closed-shop arrangements. It included the education sector, post office engineering, the BBC, higher-grade employees in the public sector generally and white-collar workers in parts of local government and certain nationalized industries. In some cases the unions concerned had adopted formal policies at conference opposing the closed shop. In others it was so controversial that, again, the ballot provisions of the 1980 Act would seem an insurmountable obstacle, and given the fact that all these are in the public sector, public obligations would preclude

employers accepting closed-shop arrangements without such ratifi-
cation. We see little room for closed-shop expansion here.

The third area, where probably the majority of employees not in
closed shops were found, covered firms and industries where unionization was limited or non-existent. These would include the wages council
sector, including such large parts of the service sector as hotels and
catering and retail distribution, agriculture and, despite a considerable
amount of union growth, banking, insurance and finance and private-
sector white-collar employment generally. A few closed shops did exist
here. But union weakness was often compounded by membership and
managerial hostility to the practice. As economic conditions in the 1980s
would seem unfavourable to a strengthening of union organization in
this area, there seems little immediate possibility of the growth of the
closed shop here.

To sum up, the evidence suggests that significant expansion of
compulsory unionism into new areas is unlikely in the 1980s. That is not
to say that no new closed shops will appear. No private-sector closed-
shop industry is completely covered by the practice and there may be,
among the myriad bargaining units found there, small groups ripe for its
introduction. Indeed a survey conducted by the Institute of Directors in
1981 revealed that a thin sprinkling of new UMAs had been introduced
since the 1980 Employment Act without recourse to a ballot. However,
such a trickle of new arrangements would not be sufficient to offset the
decline of the closed-shop population already experienced.

Possibilities of the Dismantling or Lapsing of Existing
Closed-shop Arrangements

Predicting the survival of existing closed-shop arrangements is a much
more complex task. It involves estimating the extent to which management values its closed-shop practices, especially in the more hazardous
legal environment created by the 1980 and 1982 Acts; estimating the
extent to which individuals will exert their new statutory right to non-
membership; and estimating the extent to which trade unionists will
support the closed shop, particularly as after 1 November 1984 dismissal
for non-union membership in a closed shop becomes automatically
unfair unless the arrangment has been ratified by 80 per cent of those
covered, or 85 per cent of those voting in a secret ballot.

Looking first at employer attitudes, our research in the late 1970s
discovered that management enthusiasm for the closed shop was less
than had been sometimes thought. Industrial-realations specialists

tended to be, if not indifferent, at least non-committal. This may well have been indicative of a disappointment that the closed shop had not produced the practical benefits that had been expected. Nevertheless, they tended to value it as part of the *status quo* and thus were not keen to see it removed, although this in turn may have been due to their relatively short experience of the practice and of the fact that no opportunity had arisen for the practice to operate against management interests.

Have the 1980s brought a significant managerial reassessment? Fragmentary evidence suggests that the sharp downturn in the economy has caused some managerial reappraisal of industrial relations generally. The rise in unemployment, although it began to accelerate in the 1970s, only saw a significant shift in bargaining power towards employers in the present decade. Consequently policies and procedures designed to cope with strong trade unionism through joint regulation were bound to come under scrutiny as management saw an opportunity to reassert its prerogative. The closed shop would seem particularly vulnerable in this respect on three grounds. First, while industrial-relations specialists may have convinced their companies of pragmatic reasons for its acceptance, it is probably unpopular among directors and managers generally on philosophical grounds.

Second, even industrial-relations specialists may feel able to dispense with it because it has not delivered the substantial benefits they had once expected. Where substantial costs are attributed to the practice the pressure to undermine it may be even more intense. Already we have seen how even the long-standing and supposedly robust pre-entry practices in the docks, shipping and printing have been threatened by technological change and employer avoidance strategies (Chapter 3).

If future experience teaches management that their post-entry closed shops can also impose significant costs, then they too might come under attack. In Chapter 6 we cited the example of a number of employers whom, when faced with a strike in which the unions threatened to wield the closed-shop weapon, successfully countered it by repudiating or stating their intention to repudiate their UMAs. In later 1978 the Bakers' Federation revoked its post-entry agreement with the Bakers, Food and Allied Workers Union during a national strike partly on the grounds that the union had failed to observe the disputes procedure and therefore it felt no obligation to observe the UMA, and partly to prevent it deterring a significant number of strike breakers from staying at work. In 1981 the union decided to shelve its moves to restore the closed shop, feeling the time was not appropriate. Similarly, during disputes involving ASLEF and the NUR in 1982, British Rail announced its intention to continue employing workers stripped of union membership for refusing to answer the strike call. In the case of the NUR substantial numbers did remain at work. Afterwards the union disciplined them, although it stopped short of expulsion. Even so, British Rail's guarantee was put to the test as relatively large numbers of those disciplined, as well as others, resigned or threatened to resign from the union, some forming a breakaway union. Elsewhere, similar undertakings to that given by British Rail were promised in 1982 by British Airways during the baggage handlers' dispute at Heathrow and by British Telecom to its closed-shop workers in a dispute over privatization. Rather differently, after the TUC's Day of Action in support of a pay claim by health service workers in September 1982, some employers wrote to the Department of Employment complaining that a number of their employees covered by closed-shop arrangements would have worked that day but for threats and intimidations by trade unions. How typical this was is impossible to say. But if in the 1980s government policy prompts demonstration stoppages not directly related to company industrial relations, then this is likely to put further pressure on management's tolerance of their closed-shop arrangements.

Third, how will management react to the new legal hazards involved in operating existing closed shops? The 1980 and 1982 Acts were designed to regulate the practice mainly by giving individuals far wider grounds for opting out of trade-union membership in a closed shop than did TULR(A)A 1976. They did this by increasing the financial penalties against employers and, through the 'joinder' provisions, trade unions who in breach of these grounds dismissed people or took action short of dismissal against them and by making it automatically unfair to dismiss on the grounds of non-unionism if the closed shop had not been massively supported by those covered in a secret ballot within the previous five years. Faced with these provisions management has a number of options. One would be to disengage from closed-shop agreements to avoid any possibility of legal entanglements. Another would be to modify UMAs to comply with the law. A third would be to operate closed shops as before, passively or actively work to minimize legal intervention and accept the consequence if such intervention does occur. This latter option was, according to Weekes *et al.*, widely and successfully adopted during the Industrial Relations Act period (1971–4) when management was reported to have co-operated with trade unions to dissuade employees from claiming their statutory right not to belong to a union and to operate closed shops on an informal rather than a formal basis.[3] Such a strategy is feasible in the 1980s, particularly as no blanket right to dissociate has so far been enacted and as balloting is not legally compulsory but only becomes necessary when a dimissal takes place. However, a number of significant changes have taken place since the early 1970s that may affect management's attitude. For example, the shift in the balance of power away from the unions may offer a greater opportunity to disengage from closed shops. Between 1971 and 1974 management support was sometimes prompted by a knowledge that, whatever the law said, trade unionists would refuse to work with non-members, especially in the traditional closed-shop industries. Popular support for post-1974 UMAs is much less certain. Under present economic conditions, management may calculate that industrial action would not be taken to defend the practice; or else, companies may feel that the ballot provisions offer a ready-made test of popular support and that a failure to achieve the 80–85 per cent in favour would allow them to opt out of their closed-shop arrangements. British Rail, for instance, has been reported to be seeking a review of its compulsory membership agreements in the light of the 1982 Act and to be prepared to poll its workforce on the issue. Moreover, when the issue of ballots on existing practices was first raised in the *Code of Practice* on the closed shop,[4] the CBI said the majority of its members supported the idea of periodic reviews of the closed shop by ballot. Even so, some employers' organizations questioned the advisability of the idea. The General Council of British Shipping argued that ballots on a single employer basis were impractical in their industry, although the government did not accept this view.[5] The Engineering Employers' Federation were concerned with the industrial-relations problems that might arise from ballots. Among these might be the conflict arising because of the trade-union policy of non-co-operation with such reviews and the destabilizing effect of a poll that failed to meet the 80–85 per cent support. For instance, if, say, 75 per cent voted in favour of the closed shop, could the practice be abandoned without a backlash? Or if certain parts of the bargaining unit voted solidly in favour of compulsory unionism, although the total in favour was insufficient for legal purposes, would this lead to fragmentation of the unit as the pro-closed-shop groups demanded their own agreements.'

With the possibility of such problems management attitudes are likely to depend upon the frequency with which individuals decide to opt out of union membership in closed shops and thus raise the ballot issue. The evidence of the Industrial Relations Act and the 1974–80 period suggest that such decisions are rare. Admittedly between 1974 and 1980 individuals had little legal redress if they were sacked in such circum-

stances, which inevitably persuaded workers to accept union membership reluctantly rather than jeopardize their jobs. Yet important
in limiting the number of individual problems was also the fact that
many agreements were more liberal than the law demanded.[6] Such
agreements still exist which means that many non-unionists remain
protected and will have no reason to turn to the law. As regards existing
reluctant joiners, our managerial evidence suggested that UMAs have
some effect in promoting a membership habit. We were even told of
UMAs being signed which excluded existing non-members, yet such
protected individuals quickly volunteered to join the union even though
it became a condition of employment to stay in membership once they
opted for it. Moreover, before 1980 when a change of political control
from Labour to Conservative brought a liberalizing of UMAs to allow
new recruits to remain outside the union on any grounds of conscience
whatsoever, few if any did so. Nor was there pressure from existing
employees to extend to new exemptions to cover them.[7] This would
suggest that large-scale defections from closed-shop unions are unlikely to
occur. Yet since 1980 the incentives for resigning union membership are
far greater in terms of financial compensation (see Chapter 1), while
from 1984 in situations where the closed shop has not been reviewed by
ballot or where the practice continues despite an adverse ballot
decision in legal terms, the mere fact of dismissal of non-membership,
whatever the grounds, is sufficient to win a tribunal claim. It cannot
therefore be assumed that the law will have little effect, especially as the
publicity given to the British Rail case at the Court of Human Rights
and to the role of the Freedom Association in supporting the sacked
railwaymen has raised the level of awareness concerning individual
dissent from compulsory unionism. Nevertheless, Lewis has argued that
if closed shops are operated with toleration and flexibility, if unions co-
operate in 'red circling' rather than facing the dismissal of those that
drop out of the union, if care is taken in recruitment and induction, and
if, at the end of the day, there are grounds for dismissal other than non-
membership, then individuals may need some ingenuity to secure their
high financial compensation.[8] This may mean that closed shops will
operate on two levels. The formal UMA may become merely a statement
of a rigid closed shop that does not operate in reality, while informal
exemptions are allowed and informal methods of persuasion are used to
maintain some semblance of compulsory unionism. Where informal
practices already exist, the incentive to commit them to paper will be
considerably reduced. At BL Cars, for example, the eleven unions began to negotiate a new procedural agreement with management in

January 1982. During the negotiations they suggested that the new agreement should state that union membership should be a condition of employment and that the company should accept that it should solely use outside contractors who employed unionized labour only. BL refused to write these clauses into the new procedure because they contravened the 1980 Act and the proposed 1982 Bill. Even so, management told the unions that it did not wish to break new ground or to be difficult or provocative about union membership. Equally it wished to avoid employees provoking difficulties in order to obtain unfair dismissal. The unions for their part said they would continue checking the union cards of contract labour regardless of the proposed legislation. The result was a clause that read: 'It is accepted that it is in the mutual interests of the company and its hourly graded employees that the latter be members of an appropriate signatory union.' The closed shop was to continue informally.

Because of the stiffness of the ballot proposals, operative from late 1984, it may be that the lack of ratified closed shops will reduce the widened conscience exemptions to secondary importance as individuals will commonly be protected by the automatic claim to unfair dismissal if sacked for non-membership or qualify for compensation for action against them short of the sack. If successful ballots do occur, the key issue will be how broadly industrial tribunals interpret the phrase 'genuine objection on grounds of conscience and other deeply held personal conviction'. By June 1982 only three such claims had been brought before tribunals under the 1980 Act. In all three the decision went against the claimant, suggesting, as Hanson *et al* argue, that the phrase is intended to exclude the trivial and spiteful, that political beliefs would only be a factor if for example the union frequently called overtly political strikes, and that long periods of union membership would tell against the claimant.[9]

Yet, while the conscience exemptions may be only a minor threat to the closed shop, the balloting provisions and the attendant threat of members opting out in significant numbers in the absence of a poll may cause managers to think seriously about allowing their closed shops to lapse, especially if there is a major managerial reappraisal of the role of trade unions in their enterprises. In this case the closed shop's survival will depend on the willingness of trade unionists themselves to protect the practice by unilateral action. Although the 'joinder' provisions involve trade unions in the financial penalties resulting from unfair dismissal, this is unlikely to be as significant a problem as mobilizing membership support for the practice for several reasons. First, even if trade unions become more willing to see the issue balloted, they are bound to remain wary, even in well-supported closed shops, because to secure 80–85 per cent in favour is a daunting task. Admittedly, in some traditional closed-shop areas like coal-mining, it would probably be achieved with ease, but these are precisely the areas where individual problems are unlikely to occur because the habit of trade-union membership is so deeply ingrained. Elsewhere traditions are not so strong, however. Recently negotiated UMAs, the 'paper' closed shops, were generally introduced without a ballot and the degree of popular support for them is largely unknown. During our research we attempt to rectify this lack of information, but access was difficult in 1979 because with a newly elected Conservative government pledged to legislate against the closed shop, both managers and unions were a little reluctant to see the issue raised among the workforce. Certainly in such areas it would be difficult for union representatives to protect the closed shop without substantial membership support if they encountered man-agerial reluctance to help and a significant number of individual dissenters. Despite the 'conscript army' jibe, union officials cannot force members to vote for the closed shop in a secret ballot, nor can they force members to take industrial action to preserve the practice. Both moves would be likely to be counter-productive. So what estimates can we make about popular support for the practice in these new areas?

Opinion polls tell us that even among trade unionists there is substantial hostility towards the closed shop (see Chapter 4). Hence it is safe to say that generating pro-closed-shop activity will be problematical for the unions, especially as in the current economic climate workers are generally more reluctant to take industrial action. Nevertheless, it would be dangerous to assume that such activity would be impossible to stimulate. There is an important difference between attitudes expressed to an opinion poll interviewer about the closed shop in principle and the emotions felt when 'free riders' are encountered at work, or when fellow unionists resign from the union and cross picket lines. Our own view is that trade unionists' attitudes to non-members are not constant. They vary with the kind of problems that the union encounters. It cannot be taken for granted that because recent UMAs often cover workers who may not feel particularly strongly about non-unionism, then that will remain the case. We have pointed to the symbolic importance of the closed shop to many union activists, quite apart from any practical benefits deriving from it. During periods of tension and conflict, such symbolism may permeate throughout the rank and file. For example, a management attempt to dismantle the closed shop may itself be regarded by union members as symbolic of a wider attempt to undermine the trade union and they might be moved to prevent it. The contention here is not that the closed shop will create a solidarity out of nothing and therefore have a significant effect on industrial relations in a turbulent period, but that the solidarity generated by such a period may in some circumstances help to preserve the practice. We doubt very much whether compulsory unionism in itself is capable of shaping the behaviour of large numbers of workers who over particular issues wish to defy union instructions, as the bakers' and railwaymen's experience showed. Yet workers who learn solidarity through experience of conflict may, as in the traditional areas, translate it into a strong attachment to the closed-shop principle which may so far be lacking where modern UMAs operate. In short, as we suggested in Chapter 1, it is impossible to isolate the closed shop from its industrial-relations environment. The industrial-relations problems and issues thrown up by the 1980s, particularly if the economy begins to revive and a measure of trade-union confidence is restored, will have a more significant impact on the future of the practice than the niceties of law. Certainly the closed shop is vulnerable. Even the hitherto strong pre-entry practices face fundamental challenges from new technology and employer evasion, while the latter-day post-entry arrangements have yet to prove their robustness in the face of perhaps managerial disappointment that they have not had the disciplining effect on the workforce that was once hoped. Yet the demise of the closed shop is not inevitable.

One final point is this. Our research covered a period in which one of the first significant developments was British Rail's acceptance in 1969 of the closed shop on the grounds that it was likely to help union officials keep discipline among their members and curb unofficial strikes. It ended in 1982 with British Rail threatening to repudiate the closed shop on the grounds that it was likely to help union officials keep discipline among their members during an official strike. By 1992 somebody may be undertaking another comprehensive survey of the practice in the UK. It could take courage to predict in what condition they will find the British Rail closed shop.

Notes and References

1 THE CLOSED SHOP: DEBATE, POLICY AND THE PURPOSE OF THIS BOOK

1. W. E. J. McCarthy, *The Closed Shop in Britain*, Blackwell, Oxford, 1964.
2. C. Hanson, S. Jackson and D. Miller, *The Closed Shop*, Gower Press, Aldershot, 1982, p. 15.
3. *Trade Union Immunities*, Cmnd 8128, HMSO, London, 1981, para. 263.
4. The Rt Hon. Norman Tebbit, speech to the Conservative Party Conference, Brighton, 7 October 1982.
5. J. Burton, 'Are Trade Unions a Public Good/"Bad"? The Economics of the Closed Shop', in *Trade Unions: Public Goods or Public 'Bads'?*, Institute of Economic Affairs Readings no. 17, 1978; see also J. Burton, *The Trojan Horse: Union Power in British Politics*, Adam Smith Institute, London, 1979; and F. A. Hayek, *1980s Unemployment and the Unions*, Hobart Paper 87, Institute of Economic Affairs, 1980.
6. Royal Commission on Trade Unions and Employers' Associations, Minutes of Evidence 17, Witness. The National Union of Railwaymen, Verbal Evidence, 18 January 1966, HMSO, London, 1966, para. 2606
7. L. J. McFarlane, *The Right to Strike*, Pelican, 1981, p. 49, quoting from R. and E. Frow and M. Katanka, *Strikes: A Documentary History*, Charles Knight, Croydon, 1971, p. 55.
8. C. Rose, 'Reviewing the Closed Shop in the Light of the Act', *Personnel Management*, October 1980, pp. 32–5.
9. In *New Society*, 15 February 1979, pp. 353–4.
10. J. Gennard and S. Dunn, 'The Closed Shop in British Industry', mimeo, Report to the Department of Employment, March 1983. A copy was deposited by the Secretary of State for Employment in the House of Commons Library, see Hansard, 22 March 1983, Written Answers, Column 362.
11. See J. Gennard, S. Dunn and M. Wright, 'The Content of British Closed Shop Agreements', *Department of Employment Gazette*, November 1979; J. Gennard, S. Dunn and M. Wright, 'The Extent of the Closed Shop in British Industry', *Department of Employment Gazette*, January 1980; J. Gennard, M. Gregory and S. Dunn, 'Throwing the Book', *Department of Employment Gazette*, June 1980; S. Dunn, 'The Growth of the Post-entry Closed Shop in Britain since the 1960s: Some Theoretical Considerations', *British Journal of Industrial Relations*, November 1981.
12. See McCarthy, *The Closed Shop in Britain*, pp. 212–14 and the insert on the dedication page.
13. See *Report of the Royal Commission on Trade Unions and Employers' Associations*, Cmnd 3623, HMSO, London, 1968, para. 598.
14. Ibid, para. 618.

2 THE CLOSED-SHOP PATTERN: MID-1978

1. See W. E. J. McCarthy, *The Closed Shop in Britain*, Blackwell, Oxford, 1964, ch. 1, p. 9.
2. The authors would like to express their thanks to all the individuals and organizations that co-operated in this exercise. Needless to say, these individuals and organizations are not responsible for any of the views expressed in this book.
3. The authors would like to express their thanks to the EEF for their kind and generous assistance in this exercise.
4. We would like to express our thanks in this respect to W. Brown and M. Hart of the Social Science Research Council's Industrial Relations Research Unit at the University of Warwick, and to S. Harrison from the Nuffield Centre for National Health Studies located at the University of Leeds.
5. 'Employees in Employment at June 1978', *Department of Employment Gazette*, October 1978.
6. This section is a brief survey of the main findings which have been published elsewhere. See J. Gennard, S. Dunn and M. Wright, 'The Extent of the Closed Shop in British Industry', *Department of Employment Gazette*, January 1980.
7. Our estimate of the closed-shop population in mid-1978 has been criticized by Helen Jackson as being a serious underestimate of the actual total. See H. Jackson, 'The Scope of the Closed Shop', *New Statesman*, 16 May 1980; and H. Jackson, 'The 7m Workers Who Have No Choice', *The Free Nation*, April 1981. For a brief reply, see letter by J. Gennard, S. Dunn and M. Gregory to *New Statesman*, 23 May 1980. However, fieldwork conducted in 1980 as part of the workplace industrial relations survey provided an estimate of the closed-shop population that did not differ significantly from our results. See W. W. Daniel and N. Millward, *Workplace Industrial Relations in Britain*, Heinemann, 1983, ch. III. In addition, the estimates of the closed-shop population in manufacturing provided by the Industrial Relations Research Unit at Warwick also accord with our figures. See W. Brown (ed.), *The Changing Contours of British Industrial Relations*, Blackwell, Oxford, 1981.
8. The relative increase in the closed-shop population in these industries was also found by a survey undertaken in 1977 by the SSRC Industrial Relations Research Unit at the University of Warwick. Their figures were as follows: food, drink and tobacco a rise in coverage from 4 per cent of the workforce to 35 per cent; in chemicals from 7 per cent to 27 per cent; and in clothing and footwear from 6 per cent to 16 per cent. An exact comparison between the Warwick study and our own is not possible because the former survey often used a combination of SICs. See W. Brown (ed.), *The Changing Contours of British Industrial Relations*, Blackwell, Oxford, 1981, ch. 4.
9. See McCarthy, *The Closed Shop in Britain*, p. 32.
10. The predominance of the closed shop among manual workers was confirmed in the Warwick study which found that for manual workers closed shops occurred in 29 per cent of all of the establishments surveyed but for non-manual in only 6 per cent. See Brown (ed.), *The Changing Contours of British Industrial Relations*, ch. 4, p. 55 and 56.

11. For a detailed explanation of the point, see J. Gennard, S. Dunn and M. Wright, 'The Extent of the Closed Shop in British Industry', *Department of Employment Gazette*, January 1980.

12. For example, the labour supply pre-entry closed shop operated by the National Graphical Association in national newspapers is formally contained in Rule 48 on p. 34 of the Rules of the London Region of the National Graphical Association, 1981.

13. See B. Weekes *et al.*, *Industrial Relations and the Limits of the Law*, Blackwell, Oxford, 1975, ch. 2.

14. See, for example, C. Hanson *et al.*, *The Closed Shop*, Gower Press, Aldershot 1982, ch. 7, p. 80; and J. Burton, *The Trojan Horse: Union Power in British Politics* Adam Smith Institute, London, 1979.

15. See, for example, S. Parker *et al.*, *Workplace Industrial Relations, 1972*, HMSO, London, 1974.

16. For a full discussion of the point, see J. Gennard, S. Dunn and M. Wright, 'The Content of British Closed Shop Agreements', *Department of Employment Gazette*, November 1979.

17. For example, between 1969 and 1971 five nationalized industries introduced formal closed-shop agreements while a number of others were interrupted by the Industrial Relations Act 1971. But once legal obstacles were removed the process that had been working well before 1971 was resumed and reached a peak in 1976 when twenty-two formal closed-shop agreements were newly introduced into nationalized industries or reactivated or modified in the light of TULR(A)A 1976.

18. Demands for industry-wide closed shops have been made for example by unions in wool textiles, local government, public road passenger transport, hosiery and knitwear and clothing, all without success.

19. The best example of a formal industry-wide post-entry closed shop is that found in footwear which was signed in February 1976. Our survey also revealed a similar agreement in the plant-baking industry but this was ended by the employers in 1978 following an industrial dispute. Formal pre-entry closed shops on industrial-wide bases were found in merchant shipping and acting. However, in addition a number of informal industry-wide pre-entry closed shops existed via formal rules in a union rule book.

20. This section is a brief summary of the main findings. For a more detailed study of our findings in this area, see Gennard, Dunn and Wright, 'The Content of British Closed Shop Agreements'.

21. The total number of actual formal closed-shop agreements probably numbers several thousands The survey of EEF affiliated establishments, for example, produced nearly 2000 agreements. We must stress, therefore, that we do not wish to create the impression that only 136 agreements exist in the whole of British industry.

22. Until the second half of the 1960s the typical formal closed-shop arrangement occupied a single clause in a works agreement and was encapsulated in a single sentence that read 'It is a condition of employment that all hourly paid employees become and remain members of the union.' Little or nothing was mentioned about exceptions to the rule, about how new employees or existing non-members were to be recruited to the union nor about the problems of lapsing, and of expulsion or exclusion from the union.

3 THE PRE-ENTRY CLOSED SHOP

1. For a more detailed description of the enforcement of the closed shop in merchant shipping, see Commission on Industrial Relations, Report no. 30, *Approved Closed Shop Agreement: British Shipping Federation/National Union of Seamen*, HMSO, London, 1972.
2. This trend had first began soon after the end of the Second World War. See R. L. Rowen, H. R. Northrup and M. J. Immediata, 'International Enforcement of Union Standards in Ocean Transport', *British Journal of Industrial Relations*, November 1977.
3. The question of payment to Asians on ships flying the UK flag received public attention in the immediate aftermath of the successful recapture of the Falkland Islands in June 1982. Many people were shocked when they realized that seamen who had returned from the war as heroes were rejoining the ranks of the unemployed and being replaced by Asians whose wages were less than a quarter of the rates for members of the National Union of Seamen. When the *Canberra*, which acted as the main troopship in the Falkland Islands task force, resumed merchant navy duties over half its crew were Asian and 400 UK seamen who had served on *Canberra* during its troopship duties were declared redundant.
4. This campaign first began nearly thirty years ago and is described in detail in R. L. Rowan, H. R. Northrup and M. J. Immediata, 'The International Enforcement of Union Standards in Ocean Transport', *British Journal of Industrial Relations*, November 1977.
5. These are the Main Register, the Probationary Register, the Temporary Register and the Seasonal Register.
6. Felixstowe is perhaps the most notable example here. Others include Shoreham which gained a large amount of wine trade from London; Ramsgate, which could not provide fifteen hours' work a week for twenty men in 1959, but became the main port of entry for Volkswagen cars; and Whitby, which has developed a thriving cargo trade.
7. See David F. Wilson, *Dockers: The Impact of Technological Change*, Fontana/Collins, London, 1972, p. 142.
8. The blacking of containers by dockers resulted in employers and other groups of workers taking action against the main docking union – the T&GWU – under the Industrial Relations Act 1971. These actions eventually resulted in five dockworkers being sent to prison for contempt of court and the TUC urged its affiliated unions to call a one-day general strike. In the face of these pressures the dockers were released.
9. See report of a panel of investigation into current difficulties affecting the T&GWU, the Dagenham Cold Store and F. J. Robertson Ltd, *Advisory Conciliation and Arbitration Service*, Report no. 2, March 1975, p. 8.
10. See W. E. J. McCarthy, *The Closed Shop in Britain*, Blackwell, Oxford, 1964, pp. 38–42.
11. See, for example, Royal Commission on the Press, Industrial Relations in the National Newspaper Industry, *A Report by the Advisory, Conciliation and Arbitration Service*, Research Series 1, Cmnd 6680, HMSO, London,

December 1976; and R. Martin, *Technological Change and Industrial Relations in Fleet Street,* Clarendon Press, Oxford 1981.

12. See Rules 5(5), 34 and 35 of *The Rules of the National Graphical Association,* 1982.

13. Rule 43 of the NGA is entitled *Work from Unrecognized Offices* and states: 'A member shall not perform any work that has either been received from or is going to an unrecognized office. In no circumstances shall any matter produced in an unrecognized office or matter which is likely to assist an antagonistic employer be handled by a member of the Association except by permission of the National Council in consultation with the branch or branches concerned.'

14. The 'white-card' procedure is a system whereby a card (white coloured) is issued to the member at the top of the vacancy list. The card is not issued to the second person on the list until it has been returned by the first person. Under no circumstances is a member of the former SLADE to write to or contact or approach a firm in any manner until he has received from the Branch Secretary a card of introduction (white card) to the FoC or telegram to the same effect and has contacted the father of the chapel and received a reply. In the NGA it is only *notified* vacancies that must be filled through the medium of the call book. In other words, individual members do fill unnotified vacancies without going through the call book procedure. Unnotified vacancies arise from the informal communication channels in the NGA London region.

15. The Society of Graphical and Allied Trades (1982) came into being in July 1982 when SOGAT (1975) amalgamated with the National Society of Operative Printers, Assistants and Media Personnel (NATSOPA).

16. For a fuller discussion of these strategies, see J. Gennard and S. Dunn, 'The Impact of New Technology on the Structure and Organisation of Craft Unions in the Printing Industry', *The British Journal of Industrial Relations,* March 1983.

17. See *Report of Inquiry into Certain Trade Union Recruitment Activities,* Cmnd 7706, HMSO, London, 1979.

4 THE GROWTH OF THE POST-ENTRY CLOSED SHOP SINCE THE MID-1960S: THEORETICAL FRAMEWORK

1. For a longer discussion of the issues raised in this chapter, see S. Dunn, 'The Growth of the Post-entry Closed Shop in Britain since the 1960s: Some Theoretical Considerations', *British Journal of Industrial Relations,* November 1981.

2. W. E. J. McCarthy, *The Closed Shop in Britain,* Blackwell, Oxford, 1964. McCarthy did note certain instances in which employers took the initiative in establishing closed shops, but their motives were less concerned with procuring advantages from the practice than with expressing their ideological attachment to the trade-union movement. The major examples were the Co-operative Societies and certain Labour-controlled local authorities.

3. Ibid, p. 91.

4. Ibid, p. 82.

5. McCarthy made a strong connection between the closed shop and strike activity. For example, in discussing mainly open industries, he suggested that wherever there was a factory with a number of closed shops, the chances were that the workers involved were more strike prone than average. Ibid, p. 118.

6. During the second half of the 1960s the annual percentage increase in the index of retail prices began to climb towards the 10 per cent mark. In the mid-1970s it accelerated spectacularly towards the 30 per cent level, slowly dropped back to 10 per cent by 1978, then rose again steadily towards the 20 per cent mark by the end of the decade. During the 1960s unemployment grew to a yearly average of 2.5 per cent in the years 1967–70. It continued to rise, with fluctuations, to 4.2 per cent in 1975 and to over 6 per cent by 1978. (*Source: Department of Employment Gazette.*)

7. Statutory incomes policy was in force in 1966–70 and 1972–4. Voluntary incomes policy operated, sometimes with background sanctions, in 1964–6, 1970–2, and 1974–9. Legislation regarded as hostile to themselves by trade unions was proposed by the Labour government's White Paper *In Place of Strife*, Cmnd 3888, HMSO, London, 1969, and in its Industrial Relations Bill 1970. Such legislation appeared on the statute books in the Conservative's 1971 Industrial Relations Act and, at the end of the period, in the 1980 Employment Act.

8. See, for example, P. Dubois, 'New Forms of Industrial Conflict', in volume 2 of C. Crouch and A. Pizzorno (eds), *The Resurgence of Class Conflict in Western Europe since 1968*, 2 vols, Macmillan, London, 1978, pp. 1–34. Comparing the periods 1958–67 and 1968–73, he found that in the UK a 12 per cent rise in the annual number of strikes reported, a 56 per cent rise in the number of workers involved and a 242 per cent rise in days lost. Between 1970 and 1979 an average of 12.9 million working days were lost per year through strikes, as compared to 3.3 million per year in the 1950s and 3.5 million in the 1960s. *Source*: C. J. B. Smith, R. Clifton, P. Makeham, C. Creigh and R. Burn, *Strikes in Britain*, Department of Employment, Manpower Paper no. 15, HMSO, London, 1978 and *Department of Employment Gazette.*)

9. McCarthy, *The Closed Shop in Britain*, p. 115.

10. Ibid, p. 91.

11. See, for example, B. Weekes, 'Law and the Practice of the Closed Shop', *The Industrial Law Journal*, December 1976; and M. Hart, 'Why Bosses Love the Closed Shop', *New Society*, 15 February 1979, pp. 352–4.

12. C. Hanson, S. Jackson and D. Miller, *The Closed Shop*, Gower Press, Aldershot, 1982, pp. 79–80.

13. The closed shop has generally only been of passing interest to those arguing the corporatist theme. But its spread has nevertheless been identified as a manifestation of the corporatist trend; see, for example, C. Crouch, *Class Conflict and the Industrial Relations Crisis*, Heinemann Educational Books, London, 1977.

14. Royal Commission on Trade Unions and Employers' Associations Report, Cmnd 3623, HMSO, London 1968 (Donovan Report).

15. For the extent of this development, see W. A. Brown (ed.), *The Changing*

Contours of British Industrial Relations, Blackwell, Oxford, 1981; and W. A. Brown, R. Ebsworth and M. Terry, 'Factors Shaping Shop Steward Organisation in Britain', *British Journal of Industrial Relations*, July 1978.

16. Hart, 'Why Bosses Love the Closed Shop'.
17. Dunn, 'The Growth of the Post-entry Closed Shop in Britain since the 1960s', p. 279.
18. Royal Commission on Trade Unions and Employers' Associations Report, para. 602.
19. Dunn, 'The Growth of the Post-entry Closed Shop in Britain since the 1960s', p. 283.
20. Hart, 'Why Bosses Love the Closed Shop'.
21. The Trade Union and Labour Relations Act 1974.
22. Hanson *et al.*, *The Closed Shop*, p. 80.
23. A gap in the immunities that affected closed-shop arrangements was discovered as recently as 1964 (*Rookes* v. *Barnard*) but was quickly plugged by the 1965 Trades Disputes Act.
24. The main cases were *Reynolds* v. *Shipping Federation* (1924) and *Crofter Harris Tweed* v. *Veitch* (1942).
25. See, for example, Hanson *et al.*, *The Closed Shop*, pp. 23–6; and R. Lewis and B. Simpson, *Striking a Balance*, Martin Robertson, Oxford, 1981, pp. 18–80.
26. See B. Weekes, M. Mellish, L. Dickens and J. Lloyd, *Industrial Relations and the Limits of the Law*, Blackwell, Oxford, 1975, ch. 2.
27. Ibid.
28. McCarthy, *The Closed Shop in Britain*, p. 214; quoted in Hanson *et al.*, *The Closed Shop*, p. 25.
29. McCarthy, *The Closed Shop in Britain*, p. 80.
30. Ibid, pp. 82–3.
31. Hanson *et al. The Closed Shop*, pp. 81–5.
32. Ibid, p. 84.
33. For a longer discussion of this point, see Dunn, 'The Growth of the Post-entry Closed Shop in Britain since the 1960s', pp. 289–91.
34. See Hart, 'Why Bosses Love the Closed Shop'.
35. Contained in a variety of management pamphlets and booklets; for example, S. Sweeney and D. Gill, *Closed Shop Agreements*, Institute of Personnel Management, 1976, and in circulars distributed by employers' associations.
36. E. Batstone, I. Boraston and S. Frenkel, *Shop Stewards in Action*, Blackwell, Oxford, 1977.
37. Ibid, p. 253.
38. B. Weekes, 'Law and the Practice of the Closed Shop', *Industrial Law Journal*, December 1976, p. 216.
39. See J. Gennard, S. Dunn and M. Wright, 'The Content of British Closed Shop Agreements', *Department of Employment Gazette*, November 1979, pp. 1088–92.

5 THE GROWTH OF THE POST-ENTRY CLOSED SHOP SINCE THE MID-1960S: EXPLANATIONS

1. See W. E. J. McCarthy, *The Closed Shop in Britain*, Blackwell, Oxford, 1964, p. 167; and The Royal Commission on Trade Unions and Employers' Associations, Minutes of Evidence 11, *The Gas Council*, HMSO, London, 1965, para. 1803.
2. McCarthy, *The Closed Shop in Britain*, pp. 53–4 and 115–19.
3. Ibid, p. 57.
4. For a detailed discussion on railway pay problems, see P. Bagwell, *The Railwaymen*, vol. 2, Allen & Unwin, London, 1982, ch. 5.
5. See C. McCleod, *All Change: Railway Industrial Relations in the Sixties*, Gower Press, Aldershot 1970.
6. Ibid.
7. National Board of Prices and Incomes, Report no. 8, *Pay and Conditions of Service of British Railways Staff*, Cmnd 2873, 1966.
8. See McCleod, *All Change*.
9. R. Pryke, *The Nationalised Industries*, Martin Robertson, Oxford 1980, p. 35.
10. See 'The Chronicle', *British Journal of Industrial Relations*, March 1968, November 1968 and July 1969.
11. See Pryke, *The Nationalised Industries*, ch. 9.
12. See Bagwell, *The Railwaymen*, p. 201.
13. The Royal Commission on Trade Unions and Employers' Associations, Minutes of Evidence 17, *The National Union of Railwaymen*, HMSO, London, 1966, para. 2606.
14. Ibid, Written Evidence, para. 136.
15. M. Moran, *The Union of Post Office Workers: A Study in Political Sociology*, Macmillan, London, 1974, pp. 56–7.
16. Union of Post Office Workers, *A Claim for Compulsory Trade Union Membership*, 1969.
17. Reported in the above claim.
18. Interview, the National Freight Corporation, 1 August 1978.
19. See Bagwell, *The Railwaymen*, p. 201.
20. Union of Post Office Workers, 'A Claim for Compulsory Trade Union Membership,' p. 4.
21. The Royal Commission on Trade Unions and Employers' Associations, Minutes of Evidence 5, *London Transport Board*, HMSO, London 1966, para. 910.
22. Ibid, Minutes of Evidence 14, *British Railways Board*, HMSO, London, 1966, para. 2130.
23. Moran, *The Union of Post Office Workers*, p. 79.
24. See Bagwell, *The Railwaymen*, pp. 372–7.
25. Union of Post Office Workers, 'A Claim for Compulsory Trade Union Membership', p. 11.
26. Quoted in Bagwell, *The Railwaymen*, p. 203.
27. During the Industrial Relations Act period one union in the nationalised sector, the British Association of Colliery Managers, made use of agency shop provisions in the Act.

28. See Bagwell, *The Railwaymen*, p. 203.
29. Interview with British Airways, 9 August 1978.
30. These comments were collected from interviews conducted during 1978 with: British Airways, British Steel, British Shipbuilders, British Gas, British Transport Docks Board, National Bus Company, and the National Water Board.
31. R. Undy, V. Ellis, W. E. J. McCarthy and A. M. Halmos, *Change in Trade Unions*, Hutchinson, London, 1981.
32. This late period of activity was partly due to the imminence of the Conservative government's tightening of the law on closed shops. The chief successes were achieved in Scotland and in English authorities where Labour had gained control in the immediate past.
33. McCarthy, *The Closed Shop in Britain*, p. 61.
34. Ibid, p. 168.
35. This is still the case with teachers. The majority of rank and file members of the National Union of Teachers and the National Association of Schoolteachers/Union of Women Teachers are opposed to the closed shop on principle and support the view that it is the right of teachers to belong to a union of their choice or to no union at all. The matter of the closed shop has been discussed on a number of occasions at the Annual Conference of the NAS/UWT but on every occasion the Conference has reiterated a policy of opposition to the closed shop for teachers. The NUT policy has been unaltered for over thirty years and stems from an Annual Conference decision taken in the early 1950s during its dispute at that time with the Durham County Council which decided to introduce a policy that *all* its employees must belong to a union. The NUT took industrial action to get the Council decision rescinded – an action that was eventually successful. In the early 1970s the Educational Institute of Scotland, which organizes schoolteachers in Scotland, debated the closed shop at its Annual General Meeting and decided it should be supported in principle. However there have been no moves within the Institute's membership to move towards union membership agreements. In the National Association of Teachers in Further and Higher Education there has been no particular pressures within for the introduction of the closed shop. The question of the closed shop was referred to the NATFHE National Executive in 1977. At its 1978 Annual Conference the Executive recommended that no action should be taken on the closed-shop issue. This recommendation was accepted by Conference.
36. See Undy et al., *Change in Trade Unions*, pp. 225–33.
37. M. Terry, 'Organising a Fragmented Workforce: Shop Stewards in Local Government', *British Journal of Industrial Relations*, March 1982, p. 9.
38. Ibid, p. 2.
39. The Fire Brigades Union has formal UMAs with the Greater London Council; the West Midlands, South Yorkshire and Tyne and Wear Metropolitan Counties; the Cleveland and Durham Non-Metropolitan Counties; and the Strathclyde and Central Regional Councils in Scotland.
40. See R. Fryer, A. Fairclough and T. Manson, 'Organisation and Change in the National Union of Public Employees', NUPE, 1974, quoted in Terry, 'Organising a Fragmented Workforce'.

41. Terry, 'Organising a Fragmented Workforce'.
42. E. Batstone, I. Boraston and S. Frenkel, *Shop Stewards in Action*, Blackwell, Oxford, 1977.
43. For example, a 1975 BBC television documentary in the *Inside Story* series (entitled 'The Depot') graphically illustrated the degree to which ex-miners brought their trade-union principles into the ambulance service in Sunderland.
44. See the *Glasgow Herald*, 9 March 1979; and *The Scotsman*, 6 June 1979.
45. McCarthy, *The Closed Shop in Britain*, p. 52.
46. William Brown (ed.), *The Changing Contours of British Industrial Relations*, Blackwell, Oxford, 1981, ch. 7, p. 118.
47. M. Hart, 'Why Bosses Love the Closed Shop', *New Society*, 15 February 1979.
48. See, for example, J. Goodman, E. Armstrong, J. Davis and A. Wagner, *Rule Making and Industrial Peace: Industrial Relations in the Footwear Industry*, Croom Helm, London, 1977.
49. Hart, 'Why Bosses Love the Closed Shop'.
50. See, J. Gennard, S. Dunn and M. Wright, 'The Content of British Closed Shop Agreements', *Department of Employment Gazette*, November 1979, pp. 1088–92.
51. McCarthy, *the Closed Shop in Britain*, p. 1.
52. Batstone *et al.*, *Shop Stewards in Action*; see discussion in previous chapter.

6 THE OPERATION OF THE POST-ENTRY CLOSED SHOP: IMPACT ON MANAGEMENT AND INDUSTRIAL RELATIONS

1. M. Hart, 'Why Bosses Love the Closed Shop', *New Society*, 15 February 1979.
2. S. Dunn *et al.*, 'The Closed Shop in Engineering' mimeo, London School of Economics, 1979.
3. Hart, 'Why Bosses Love the Closed Shop'.
4. B. Weekes *et al.*, *Industrial Relations and the Limits of the Law*, Blackwell, Oxford, 1975.
5. See S. Sweeney and D. Gill, *Closed Shop Agreements*, Institute of Personnel Management, 1976.
6. Hart, 'Why Bosses Love the Closed Shop'.
7. The remainder did not reply to one or other or both of the questions asked.
8. Unlike in the EEF survey, these responses are unaffected by non-repliers.
9. In banking, footwear, textiles, engineering and the nationalized industries, examples were found of unions and management reporting that the closed shop had strengthened the union position by preventing the loss of membership and giving union officials more confidence to deliver unpopular agreements to employers. As one official of the NUR told us, 'the late 1960s was a period of drastic change on the railways with a major pay and efficiency deal being concluded in 1968–9. The closed shop was part of this package. Many of the provisions of the agreement were highly unpopular with the rank and file and the problem for management was that once they had got union consent, how were they to secure employee consent.'

10. As happened in the baking industry when the employers withdrew from the closed-shop agreement rather than face the possibility of having to dismiss strike breakers.
11. See *Guide on Trade Union Organization and the Closed Shop*, TUC, February 1979, para. 13, p. 20.
12. See *TUC Congress Report*, 1978, pp. 458–62.
13. See *Disputes Principles and Procedures*, TUC, December 1979, p. 8.
14. See, for example, W. Brown, *Piecework Bargaining*, Heinemann, London, 1973; W. Brown, 'A Consideration of Custom and Practice, *British Journal of Industrial Relations*, March 1972; D. Miller and W. Form. *Industrial Sociology*, Harper & Row. New York, 1964, ch. 15; S. B. Mathewson, *Restruction of Output among Unorganised Workers*, Viking Press, New York, 1931; and D. Roy, 'Quota Restruction and Gold Bricking in a Machine Shop', *American Journal of Sociology*, March 1952.
15. See F. Roethlisberger and W. Dickson, *Management and the Worker*, Harvard University Press, 1939.
16. See S. Hill, 'Norms, Groups and Power: The Sociology of Workplace Industrial Relations', *British Journal of Industrial Relations*, July 1974.

7 THE OPERATION OF THE CLOSED SHOP: THE UNION AND THE INDIVIDUAL WORKER

1. See, for example, *The Report of the Royal Commission on Trades Unions and Employers Association*, Cmnd 3638, HMSO, London, 1968; Working Papers on proposed industrial relations legislation, Department of Employment, July 1979; 'The Political and Industrial Effect of Joanna Harris', *Financial Times*, 18 April 1981; and *Proposals for Industrial Relations Legislation*, Department of Employment, November 1981, para. 4.
2. Statement by Norman Tebbit, Secretary of State for Employment, in a radio interview on LBC Radio, 17 August 1981.
3. See *Guide on Trade Union Organisation and the Closed Shop*, February 1979, Clause 16, p. 21.
4. See Prime Minister's address to Conservative Party Conference, 1979, Publicity Department, Conservative Central Office, Prime Minister/1059/79.
5. A typical clause in an agreement to cover this would be 'All the parties must be made aware that no action will be taken to dismiss an employee for failure to comply with the agreement until the company is satisfied that the person concerned has had the opportunity of exercising all rights of appeal, both within the trade union's rules and where appropriate, subsequently to the TUC Independent Review Body. It follows that there must not be adverse treatment of an employee whilst appeals procedures are being followed, or whilst notice is being served following dismissal for failure to comply with the agreement.'
6. A noticeable exception was the negotiations for a union membership agreement in the non-industrial Civil Service. However, there was an additional management sticking point in these negotiations. namely that

there had to be a ballot of the employees to be affected.

7. See for example, The Local Authorities' Conditions of Service Advisory Board, *Employee Relations Handbook*, 1977, ch. 9, Union Membership Agreements, p. 58, para. 9.34.

8. See Report of Inquiry into certain Trade Union Recruitment Activities, Cmnd 7706, HMSO, London, 1979, para. 51.

9. See *Proposals for Industrial Relations Legislation*, Department of Employment, November 1981, para. 25.

10. See *Proposals for Industrial Relations Legislation*, Department of Employment, November 1981, para. 28.

11. See Department of Employment Press Notice entitled 'Closed Shop Victims Sought', dated 28 October 1982.

12. The government's basis of this figure was that it was the one quoted by Miss Helen Jackson in an article in *The Times*, 12 August 1981.

13. Mr J. B. H. Billam was appointed on 1 November 1982 as the independent assessor. His terms of reference were 'to inquire into and report on questions arising in connection with applications for compensation made under Section 2 and Schedule 1 to the Employment Act 1982, in respect of dismissals from a closed shop between 1974 and 1980'.

14. We are grateful to the Department of Employment for the provision of this information.

15. The individual concerned was reported as saying that he did not object to the AUEW or to unions in general, but resented being forced to join the union under duress and had suffered for the decision. He also reported that he thought what had happened was distressing in that he had thought the people at the establishment were his friends but he had suffered a lot of harassment and intimidation. See *Financial Times*, 24 December 1982.

16. One received compensation of £3603; another £2904, a third £1443.50 and the fourth a payment of £2648.

17. See J. Gennard, S. Dunn and M. Gregory, 'Throwing the Book', *Department of Employment Gazette*, June 1980.

18. See *TUC Disputes Principles and Procedures*, TUC, December 1979.

19. See, for example, the case of *Huntley* v. *Thornton* in 1957, the details of which are described in W. E. J. McCarthy, *The Closed Shop in Britain*, Blackwell, Oxford, 1964, ch. 10, pp. 249f; and *Goad* v. *Amalgamated Engineering Workers Union (Engineering Section)* 1973.

20. See B. Weekes, M. Mellish, L. Dickens, and J. Lloyd, *Industrial Relations and the Limits of the Law*, Blackwell, Oxford, 1975, ch. 3, p. 70.

21. There were estimated to have been about 100 local officials who defied the strike instruction.

22. Disciplined NUR members felt their treatment was harsh, for example relative to that imposed by the engine drivers' union, ASLEF, on 417 of its 28 000 members who worked at some stage during its two-week official strike in July 1982 over the attempt by the BRB to introduce flexible rostering for engine drivers. ASLEF imposed a fine of £10 for every day worked on members who defied the official strike order. For those, therefore, who worked during the whole strike the total fine would have amounted to about £100. No problems arose from the implementation of this decision.

23. See Report of the Royal Commission on Trade Unions and Employers

Associations, Cmnd 3623, HMSO, London, 1968, paras 619−21 inclusive

24. Ibid.

25. The benefits lost included pension fund rights, unemployment benefits and death benefits. The employers claimed that in the case of two individuals the accrued worth of these benefits was of the order of £700. The management of the *Leicester Mercury* did not feel disposed to resume normal working until they had assurance that their 'loyal' employees would not be penalised to this heavy extent.

26. The TUC's proposals are stated in full in the TUC General Council Report to the 1969 TUC Congress.

27. The Donovan Commission had recommended that an independent body be established to hear complaints against trade unions by individuals who had exhausted or did not have access to the trade union's internal procedures. It was envisaged that the body would be composed of three members – two trade unionists and a lawyer acting as chairman. Awards of damages made by the review body would have been legally enforceable. However, legislation based on these proposals was dropped after the defeat of the Labour government in the general election of 1970.

28. For a full analysis of the Committee's method of operation, see K. D. Ewing and W. M. Rees, 'The TUC Independent Review Committee and the Closed Shop', *Industrial Law Journal*, June 1981.

29. The reasons for this included: the complainants had not exhausted all internal union procedures; they had been properly excluded for arrears; they had been dismissed from employment for misconduct and they had declined to join the union.

30. This time factor was given as the chief reason by the government for refusing to limit the right of the individual to complain about unreasonable exclusion or expulsion from a trade union in a closed-shop situation under the Employment Act 1980 until after voluntary procedures, including the IRC, were exhausted.

31. See L. Dickens, M. Hart, M. Jones and B. Weekes, 'Why Legislation Has Failed to Provide Employment Protection', *British Journal of Industrial Relations*, July 1982.

32. See P. Lewis, 'An Analysis of why Legislation Has Failed to Provide Employment Protection for Unfairly Dismissed Employees', *British Journal of Industrial Relations*, November 1981.

33. For example, in Docherty, Moore, Worrall and APEX, the complainants resigned from the T&GWU to join APEX following a local disagreement. When the three were accepted by APEX other T&GWU members objected, a strike followed and they were subsequently dismissed. The Committee proposed that the three be found work outside the department where they previously worked so that they would not have to rejoin their former ACTSS branch. See TUC *Congress Report*, 1978, pp. 392−5.

34. See *Code of Practice on Closed Shop Agreements and Arrangements* 1983, paras 18−23 inclusive, 54−62 inclusive.

35. See Advisory, Conciliation and Arbitration Service, *Annual Report 1981*, p. 32, para. 4.4.

8 THE CLOSED SHOP IN THE 1980: CONCLUSIONS AND PROSPECTS

1. To an extent our predictions are hampered by the fact that they were made prior to the general election of June 1983. At the time of writing the outcome of that election seemed likely to have important implications for the trade-union movement in general and the closed shop in particular. A clear Conservative victory would bring further legislation to reform the trade unions and possibly further legal curbs on the closed shop. A Labour victory, which did not appear probable, would have brought some loosening of the statutory net around the practice.
2. See M. Gregory, 'The NUJ and the Closed Shop', mimeo, unpublished MSc thesis, London School of Economics, 1979.
3. See B. Weekes *et al.*, *Industrial Relations and the Limits of the Law*, Blackwell, Oxford, 1975, ch. 2.
4. *Code of Practice on Closed Shop Agreements and Arrangements.*, Department of Employment, 1983.
5. For the reasons see Hansard, 25 March 1982, pp. 726–72.
6. See J. Gennard, S. Dunn and M. Wright, 'The Content of British Closed Shop Agreements', *Department of Employment Gazette*, November 1979.
7. For example, Derbyshire County Council, Nottinghamshire County Council in 1978 and the Greater London Council in 1979.
8. R. Lewis, 'Managing the Closed Shop: Post-Prior and Post-Tebbit', *Personnel Management*, July 1982.
9. G. Hanson *et al.*, *The Closed Shop*, Gower Press, Aldershot, 1982, pp. 90–1. For further discussion on this issue, see R. Lewis and B. Simpson, *Striking a Balance*, Martin Robertson, Oxford, 1981, pp. 87–8.

Bibliography

BOOKS

Allen, V., *Power in Trade Unions*, Longman Green, London, 1954.

Bagwell, P., *The Railwaymen*, vol. 2, Allen & Unwin, London, 1982.

Batstone, E., Boraston, I. and Frenkel, S., *Shop Stewards in Action*, Blackwell, Oxford, 1977.

Brown, W., *Piecework Bargaining*, Heinemann, London, 1973.

Brown, W. (ed.), *The Changing Contours of British Industrial Relations*, Blackwell, Oxford, 1981.

Burton, J., *The Trojan Horse: Union Power in British Politics*, Adam Smith Institute, London, 1979.

Crouch, C., *Class Conflict and the Industrial Relations Crisis*, Heinemann Educational Books, London, 1977.

Daniel, W. W. and Millward, N., *Workplace Industrial Relations in Britain*, Heinemann. Educational Books, London, 1983.

Golden, C. S. and Ruttenberg, H. J., *The Dynamics of Industrial Democracy*, Harper & Row, New York, 1942.

Goodman, J., Armstrong, E., Davis, J. and Wagner, A., *Rule Making and Industrial Peace: Industrial Relations in the Footwear Industry*, Croom Helm, London, 1977.

Hanson, C. S., Jackson S. and Miller, D., *The Closed Shop*, Gower Press, Aldershot, 1982.

Hayek, F. A., *1980s Unemployment and the Unions*, Hobart Paper 87, Institute of Economic Affairs, London, 1980.

Lewis, R. and Simpson, B., *Striking a Balance?*, Martin Robertson, Oxford, 1981.

McCarthy, W. E. J., *The Closed Shop in Britain*, Blackwell, Oxford, 1964.

McLeod, C., *All Change: Railway Industrial Relations in the Sixties*, Gower Press, Aldershot, 1970.

McFarlane, L. J., *The Right To Strike*, Pelican, Harmondsworth, 1981.

Martin R., *New Technology and Industrial Relations in Fleet Street*. Clarendon Press, Oxford, 1981.

Miller, D. and Form, W., *Industrial Sociology*, Harper & Row, New York, 1964.

Miller, R. and Wood, J. B., *What Price Unemployment? An Alternative Approach*, Hobart Paper 92. Institute of Economic Affairs, London, 1982.

Moran, M., *The Union of Post Office Workers: A Study in Political Sociology*, Macmillan, London, 1974.

Parker, S. *et al.*, *Workplace Industrial Relations*, HMSO, London, 1972.

Parkinson, J. R., *The Economics of Shipbuilding*, Cambridge University Press, Cambridge, 1960.

Pryke, R., *The Nationalised Industries*, Martin Robertson, Oxford, 1980.
Robbins, L. (ed.), *Trade Unions: Public Goods or Public 'Bads'?*, Reading 17, Institute of Economic Affairs, London, 1978.
Roethlisberger, F. and Dickson, W., *Management and Unions*, Harvard University Press, Cambridge, Mass., 1939.
Sissons, K., *Industrial Relations in Fleet Street*, Blackwell, Oxford, 1975.
Undy, R. Ellis, V. McCarthy, W. E. J. and Halmos, A. M., *Change in Trade Unions*, Hutchinson, London, 1981.
Webberburn, K. W., *The Worker and the Law*, 3rd edn, Pelican, 1971.
Weekes, B., Dickens, L., Mellish, M. and Lloyd, J., *Industrial Relations and the Limits of the Law*, Blackwell, Oxford, 1975.
Wilson, D. F., *Dockers: The Impact of Technology Change*, Fontana/Collins, London, 1972.

CHAPTERS IN BOOKS

Burton, J., 'Are Trade Unions a Public Good/Bad? The Economics of The Closed Shop', in L. Robbins, *Trade Unions: Public or Public 'Bads'?*, Reading 17, Institute of Economic Affairs, London, 1978.
Dubois, P., 'New Forms of Industrial Conflict', in C. Crouch and A. Pizzorno (eds), *The Resurgence of Class Conflict in Western Europe since 1968*, vol. 2, Macmillan, London, 1978.
Golden, C. S. and Ruttenberg, W. J., 'The Union Shop is Democratic and Necessary', in E. Wight Bakke and Clark Kerr (eds), *Union, Management and the Public*, Brace & Co., New York, 1948.
Picketts, M., 'Is Efficiency More Important than Justice and Equity', in L. Robbins (ed.), *Trade Unions: Public Goods or Public 'Bads'?*, Reading 17, Institute of Economic Affairs, London, 1978.

JOURNALS

Bennett, J. and Johnson, M., 'Free Riders in the US Labour Unions: Artifice or Affliction?', *British Journal of Industrial Relations*, July 1979.
Brown, W., 'A Consideration of "Custom and Practice"', *British Journal of Industrial Relations*, March 1972.
Brown, W., Ebsworth, R. and Terry, M., 'Factors Shaping Shop Steward Organisation in Britain', *British Journal of Industrial Relations*, July 1978.
Dickens, L., Hart, M., Jones, M. and Weekes, B., 'Why Legislation Has Failed to Provide Employment Protection', *British Journal of Industrial Relations*, July 1982.
Dunn, S., 'The Growth of the Post-entry Closed Shop in Britain since the 1960s: Some Theoretical Considerations', *British Journal of Industrial Relations*, November 1981.
Ewing, K. D. and Rees, W. M., 'The TUC Independent Review Committee and the Closed Shop', *Industrial Law Journal*, June 1981.
Gennard, J. and Dunn, S., 'The Impact of New Technology on the Structure and Organisation of Craft Unions in the Printing Industry', *British Journal of Industrial Relations*, March 1983.

Hill, S., 'Norms, Groups and Power: The Sociology of Workplace Industrial Relations', *British Journal of Industrial Relations*, July 1974.

Lewis, P., 'An Analysis of Why Legislation Has Failed to Provide Employment Protection for Unfairly Dismissed Employees', *British Journal of Industrial Relations*, November 1981.

Lewis, R., 'Managing the Closed Shop: Post Prior and Post Tebbit', *Personnel Management*, July 1982.

Rose, C., 'Reviewing the Closed Shop in the Light of the Act', *Personnel Management*, October 1980.

Rowen, R. L., Northrup, H. R. and Immediata, M. J., 'International Enforcement of Union Standards in Ocean Transport', *British Journal of Industrial Relations*, November 1977.

'Symposium: Economic Aspects of Union Membership: Free Riders or Paying Customers', *Journal of Labor Research*, Fall 1980.

Terry, M., 'Organising a Fragmented Workforce: Shop Stewards in Local Government', *British Journal of Industrial Relations*, March 1982.

Wedderburn, K. W., 'Labour Law and Industrial Relations in Britain', *British Journal of Industrial Relations*, July 1972.

OFFICIAL SOURCES

(a) Advisory Conciliation and Arbitration Service

Annual Report 1981.

Report of a Panel of Investigation into Current Difficulties affecting the T&GWU, the Dagenham Cold Store and F. J. Robertson Ltd, ACAS Report no. 2, March 1975.

(b) Commission on Industrial Relations

Report no. 30, *Approved Closed Shop Agreements: British Shipping Federation/National Union of Seamen*, HMSO, London, 1972.

Report no. 40, *Approved Closed Shop in Theatre, Independent Television and Films*, HMSO, London, 1973.

(c) Department of Employment

Code of Practice on Closed Shop Agreements and Arrangements, 1980.

Code of Practice on Closed Shop Agreements and Arrangements, 1983.

'Employees in Employment at June 1978', *Gazette*, October 1978.

Gennard, J., Dunn, S. and Wright, M., 'The Content of British Closed Shop Agreements', *Gazette*, November 1979.

Gennard, J., Dunn, S. and Wright, M., 'The Extent of the Closed Shop in British Industry', *Gazette*, January 1980.

Gennard, J., Dunn, S. and Gregory, M., Throwing the Book', *Gazette*, June 1980.

Working Papers on proposed industrial relations legislation, July 1979.

Proposals for Industrial Relations Legislation, November 1981.

(d) Green Papers

Trade Union Immunities, Cmnd 8128, HMSO, London, 1981.

(e) National Board for Prices and Incomes

Report no. 8, *Pay and Conditions of Service of British Rail Staff*, Cmnd 2873, HMSO, London, 1966.

ROYAL COMMISSIONS

(a) Press
Industrial Relations in the National Newspaper Industry: A Report by Advisory, Conciliation and Arbitration Service, Research Series 1, Cmnd 6680, HMSO, London, December 1976.

(b) Trades Unions and Employers' Associations
Report, Cmnd 3623, HMSO, London, 1968.
Minutes of Evidence, 5, *London Transport Board*, HMSO, London, 1966.
Minutes of Evidence, 11, *The Gas Council*, HMSO, London, 1965.
Minutes of Evidence, 14, *British Railways Board*, HMSO, London, 1966.
Minutes of Evidence, 17, *National Union of Railwaymen*, HMSO, London, 1966.

INQUIRIES

Report of Devlin Committee into Decasualisation and Causes of Dissension, Cmnd 2734, HMSO, London, 1965.
Report of Inquiry into Certain Trade Union Recruitment Activites, Cmnd 7706, HMSO, London, 1979.

EMPLOYER AND UNION SOURCES

Trades Union Congress, *Report* 198.
Trades Union Congress, *Disputes Principles and Procedures*, December 1979.
Trades Union Congress, *Guide on Trade Union Organisation and the Closed Shop*, February 1979.
Trades Union Congress, *Commentary on the Employment Bill*, January 1980.

OTHER

Conservative Political Centre, *A Giant's Strength*, 1958.
Economist Intelligence Unit, *Survey of the National Newspaper Industry*, 1966.
Hart, M., 'Why Bosses Love the Closed Shop', *New Society*, 15 February 1979.

Jackson, H. 'The Scope of the Closed Shop', *New Statesmen*, 16 May 1980.
Jackson, H., 'The 7m workers Who Have No Choice', *Free Nation*, April 1981.
Lewis R., Davies P. and Webberburn W., *Industrial Relations Law and the Conservative Government*, Fabian Trade Union Special, NCLC Publishing Society, October 1979.

Index